GUIDE TO SOURCES OF ENGLISH HISTORY FROM 1603 TO 1660 IN EARLY REPORTS OF THE ROYAL COMMISSION ON HISTORICAL MANUSCRIPTS

by

Eleanor Stuart Upton, Ph.D.

Second Edition

The Scarecrow Press, Inc.
New York & London   1964

Copyright 1964, by Eleanor S. Upton

L. C. Card Number 64-11782

To M. F. U.

PREFACE

The first edition of this book, published in 1952, has for some years been out of print. Meanwhile the sections: "Aids to the use of the Reports" and Appendix A, "Parliamentary proceedings, 1621 to 10 January, 1642" need to be brought up to date. These sections and the Introduction have been revised in the light of the two Reports of the Commissioners that have appeared since 1946 as well as other recent publications in the field of study with which this Guide is concerned.

The main part of the work is published practically as in the first edition. This part is the "Subject-Index, a Topical Guide to Materials in English History, 1603-1660, in collections of manuscripts represented in Reports I-IX and subsequent Reports on these collections." A considerable proportion of the index-slips for this were made by George P. Winship, Jr., who worked for nearly an academic year without compensation. However, the bulk of them are in the handwriting of the compiler, who takes full responsibility for the work as it stands.

In an earlier form and with a somewhat different scope the work was submitted as a dissertation to the University of Chicago, in the Graduate Library School. Those to whom I am indebted for advice and criticism in working out this as well as the first edition in its present form have been, above all, Wallace Notestein, but also Hartley Simpson, Thomas C. Mendenhall, the late Godfrey Davies, and the late Frances Helen Relf.

In preparing this second edition I gratefully acknowledge my indebtedness to my adviser, Mr. Mendenhall. Parts of the text of the "Aids" have kindly been edited by Roger H. Ellis, Secretary of the Historical Manuscripts Commission, and others by Miss W.D. Coates, Registrar of the National Register of Archives. The Smith College Library, particularly the Documents Division, has given much help, including facilities for work. The Hampshire Inter Library Center at the University of Massachusetts, and Forbes Library, Northampton, have also been of much assistance. As before, the patience and cooperation of the publisher, Ralph R. Shaw, are fully appreciated.

Finally, though its first line may seem somewhat dubious if applied to the indexer, Pope's couplet from the Dunciad, Book I, has provided the motto for this work:

> "How index-learning turns no student pale,
> But holds the eel of science by the tail."

E.S.U.

Hadley, Massachusetts, August, 1963.

6

CONTENTS

7

INTRODUCTION

The Reports of the Royal Commission on Historical Manuscripts describe privately-owned collections of manuscripts of historical interest. They are a mine of wealth for the historian, but a mine that is hard to work. This Guide is designed to aid in the extraction of material relating to English history between 1603 and 1660 from the first nine of these Reports, and from later Reports on collections that are dealt with in the first nine. It is further limited to collections which were in private hands in England or Wales at the time the first Report on each was made. Collections then in the possession of corporate bodies are excluded; so are all collections that are not represented in the first nine Reports. The main part of the Guide is a Subject-Index of topics other than persons and places. It gives direct references to volume and page in the Reports.

Since 1870 the Commission has been issuing these Reports on manuscripts of historical interest not in public custody, but in the possession of private persons or of certain corporate bodies. The Reports are of two kinds, those of the Commissioners themselves, which are made to the Crown at intervals, and those which they introduce, namely, the Inspectors' Reports on individual collections. We shall use the term "Report" in speaking of either kind, but it is to the Inspectors' Reports alone that the Subject-Index in this Guide refers. From 1870 to 1884 these were issued as Appendices to the First through the Ninth Report of the Commission, in folio, with the text in double columns. From 1885 to 1899 they were in separate octavo volumes, but numbered as Appendices to the Tenth through the Fifteenth Report. Since 1899 they have appeared and continue to appear as separate volumes or series, except that collections too small to fill a volume are combined in the set entitled "Various Collections." A termination has now been fixed for the publication of these separate series of volumes, as stated in the Twenty-Third Report of the Commission, 1961.

In the early folio Reports the material is in many cases so unorganized and so briefly described that one may well give up at the first look at the columns of fine print. However, a number of collections have been given a supplementary or a more systematic treatment in later Reports. Here the manuscripts are usually calendared, that is, they are placed in chronological order, and each is quoted in extenso, or in extracts, is given in abstract form, or is summarized. In order to cover each collection in the first nine Reports that contains material in our field, any Report issued since the Ninth that treats of one of these same collections is included in the

Index. The Digby collection appears in Report VIII, Appendix I, and an additional portion of it in Report X, Appendix I, so we include both. Many of the Bath manuscripts within our period in Report III (1872) were calendared in two volumes, 1904-07, so the Index gives references also to "Bath Vol. I-II."

There are indexes to each volume of the Reports, but these, especially in the folio volumes, are mainly of names of persons and places. A composite index of place-names and one of personal names have been published by the Commission, but to find much of the material on other topics there is nothing to do but read the text of the Reports.

The text of the Reports was read to make our Subject-Index. An index-slip was made for each item, that is, each manuscript or group of manuscripts that could be entered under a particular subject or category. There are no index-entries directly under names of persons or places alone. These are considered to be taken care of not only by the Commission's own indexes but also by its lists of the collections and family papers on which it has reported, given, for instance, in the Twenty-Second Report.

SELECTION OF MATERIAL

This Subject-Index, then, is a topical guide to materials on the period from 1603 to 1660 in collections represented in the first nine Reports, and in later Reports dealing with the same collections. As

for its limitation to collections which were in England
or Wales, in private hands and not in the possession
of any corporate body, at the time the first Report
on each was made, this is not only to reduce the
undertaking to manageable proportions but because in-
stitutions may be expected to provide their own guides.
A "List of Collections" giving the titles of those which
furnish the material for this Guide is added, as Appendix B. The omission of four notable collections is
due to the fact that they were in process of being
calendared while our Guide was being compiled. Our
Index gives references to any part of a series that is
completed. They are the De la Warr and the Sack-
ville collections, known together as the Knole MSS.,
the Salisbury (Cecil) MSS., and the De L'Isle and
Dudley (Penshurst) MSS. Calendars like that of the
Downshire collection, though completed before the first
edition of this Guide went to press, have been omitted
because they are not represented in Reports I-IX.
Both classes of calendars thus excluded have been
edited by scholars and have introductions and indexes
of their own, which provide a more adequate approach
than those of Reports I-IX.

The exact dates covered by this Guide are from
the accession of James I, 24 March, 1603, to the
return of Charles II, 29 May, 1660. By "English
History" within these dates is meant all aspects of
life, political, military, social, economic, cultural
and ecclesiastical, in England, Wales and the British

colonies. The history of Scotland, Ireland and the Continent is included only when considered (somewhat arbitrarily) to be inseparable from that of England. We include the Bishops' Wars with Scotland, but not internal events north of the Border; the Irish Rebellion and Civil War, but not English plantations in Ireland; the Palatinate War, but not the Seven Years' War in general. Relations with foreign nations are included, and military service of Englishmen under foreign sovereigns, but not foreign events unless reported by Englishmen nor travel abroad except by English travelers.

We omit material that is of no interest except for persons and localities, which means manorial, tenurial, heraldic and genealogical items, as well as most legal documents, appointments to military or civil offices, and scattered family letters. Many names do appear, however, in the entries under the subjects. For instance, under "Letters (collections)" we have those of Sir Abel Barker and family, and we find Bermuda under "Colonies." Many names, both of persons and places, appear in the entries under sub-headings in the section "Civil Wars, 1642-1651." Purely literary items, such as poems, are omitted, and also treatises on subjects outside the limits we have set.

For the purposes of this Guide, all manuscripts or groups of manuscripts within its scope are considered "sources," whether originals or copies, significant or trivial. We omit most of those which the Report states have been printed, but have made no attempt to trace what others may have appeared in print. Such multiple copies as tracts in manuscript, or transcripts of official documents which presumably are in published collections, are not included. Omitted are all Parliamentary proceedings, in the strict sense, between the opening of the Parliament of 1621 and 10 January, 1642. Instead there is a reference in the Subject-Index under this heading to Appendix A, where is given a selective list of Parliamentary proceedings of this period that have appeared in print.

FORM AND ARRANGEMENT

The Subject-Index is in entry-a-line form, with main heads in alphabetical order. A semicolon after the first group of words in an entry marks the termination of the main head. What follows, either on the same line or indented below, is a sub-head, the words before the semicolon being understood. The same applies to sub-sub-heads, which are introduced by an indented dash. For example:

Cloth trade; 1617,	I, 57a
export; reversion of,	II, 59b
--; to France; 1604,	III, 52b
--; --; Mar., 1604 (05),	III, 52b-53a*

Sub-heads are arranged as seems most useful, whether alphabetically, by date, logically, or haphazardly. The more inclusive or the unspecified in range of dates or subject usually come first.

14

In certain cases, such as that of the "Civil Wars,"
specific subjects are gathered under a general subject,
forming a classified catalogue of items. Usually, however, "see also" references tie together related subjects,
or else they lead from the general to the specific,
though not in reverse. If there is only one entry under
a specific subject, it appears also under the general
subject. For instance, the item on tilting appears not
only under "Tilting" but also under "Sports and games."
But if there are several entries under the specific,
they are not repeated under the general, but are
covered by a cross-reference. Under "Sports and
games" we say "See also: Hawking; Hunting," because
under each of these we have more than one entry.
Another reason for repetition in the Index is that the
same item may appear under more than one head if
it has more than one subject approach or if it contains
material on more than one subject. For instance,
"Prices; see also: Accounts (receipts and expenses)"
means that some of the items referred to under "Accounts" contain data on prices, though the word "prices"
may not appear in the entries under "Accounts."

Matters touched upon in a long document or a series
of letters cannot all be brought out under subject as
is done for isolated items. Therefore in passages in
the Reports referred to under "Letters (collections),"
"Letters of news," "Diaries, journals and memoirs,"
there will be found material on wars and other public
events in addition to the material brought out under

those subjects. Manuscripts referred to under these collective heads and under such others as "Household accounts," will of course contain material on innumerable specific subjects.

DATES, ABBREVIATIONS, SYMBOLS, PAGE-REFERENCES

The year is given as in the Reports, often omitting the month and day. Very few attempts have been made to verify dates, or to establish whether a date between 1 January and 24 March is Old Style or New Style. Therefore a year standing alone may refer to either of two consecutive years. When the double date is given, it appears for example, as 1620(21). A double day of the month, for example, 14(24) Apr., adds the day according to the Gregorian calendar. If the Report or the compiler of this Guide queries a date, it is followed by a question mark; if a date is supplied by either of them, it is enclosed in curves (parentheses). A date followed by a dash and a blank space means that the closing date before 1660 of material covering several years is not determined. For example, we have:

> Accounts (receipts and expenses)--Private; 17th cent. (early), 1620-   , III, 292b (an item reading "Several old account-books, from 1620")

> Letters (collections) of general content-- 1603-1660, 1624-   , IV, 360a (an item reading "Manuscripts, historical, 1624-1734," giving no indication of the date of the latest letter before 1660)

16

Often the inclusive dates of a series of papers as given in the Reports, and hence in the Index, do not represent their actual range but only the period covered by the items singled out by the inspector for notice.

Besides the usual abbreviations, such as "ca." for "circa," and "co." for "county" as in "co. Rutland," we use "(n. d.)" for "no date," and "temp." for "tempore" as in "temp. Jac. 1" and "temp. Car. 1" for the reigns of James I and Charles I, respectively. "Passim" after inclusive page-numbers means that there are scattered items on the subject throughout the pages cited.

Sometimes a notation such as "no. 30" or "vol. xcv" follows the page-reference. This is a designation given by the owner to his manuscript and is added in the Subject-Index to make it easier to find the item in a crowded column of fine print. If there is a date following the page-reference, it is the date of the letter or document and may not be the date of the event to which it relates.

Manuscript items described in the Reports with such exasperating brevity as "a bundle of letters" are not of much use unless the originals can be seen. Many, however, are given with sufficient fullness to supply matter for research, especially if the manuscripts themselves may not be available. We have attempted, doubtless inconsistently, to point out items given with essential fullness in the Reports by placing an asterisk after the page-reference in the Subject-Index. This applies not only to isolated items, but also to a series, for instance of letters, if a fair proportion is given full treatment in the Report.

An asterisk after a particular page-reference applies also to any other page-reference to the same volume that may precede it. It does not apply to any page-numbers that follow the asterisk. In the example; Progresses, royal; of James I, V, 295b, 407b*; VI, 324a*, 456b, the two items in Volume V are given fully, and the first one in Volume VI is given fully, but the second in Volume VI is not. We repeat the volume-number when the page-reference for a sketchily-reported item precedes instead of following the page-reference for one given full treatment. An example is Palatinate; James I and, 1622-1623, VIII (1), 94b (no. 7); VIII (1), 214a-215b, passim*. The item on 94b is not treated as fully as the items scattered from 214a to 215b.

In giving page-references the number of the Report is in roman numerals and the number of the Appendix, if any, is in curves (parentheses) after it. If there is only one Appendix, no appendix-number is given. Reports published as separate volumes are referred to under the title of the collection or series, for instance, "Rutland MSS.," "Var.Coll." (Various Collections). The following are examples.

> II, 44a (vol. xcv)   meaning Second Report,
> Appendix, page 44, column 1, a MS.

numbered "vol. xcv"

III, 194a and Bath MSS., Vol. I, 1-6*
meaning Third Report, Appendix, page
194, column 1, and the separate volume
"Bath MSS.," Vol. I, pages 1-6 (the same
item in both the Third Report and the
Bath MSS., but fully treated in the Bath
MSS. volume only)

VIII(2), 50a, b meaning Eighth Report, Appendix II, page 50, column 1 and column 2
(two separate items)

IX(2), 394a-b* meaning Ninth Report,
Appendix II, page 394, columns 1 and
2 (one item, continuous, fully treated)

Rutland MSS., Vol. IV, 454-540, passim*
meaning MSS. of the Duke of Rutland,
Vol. IV, 1911, pages 454-540 (scattered
items, fully treated)

IX(2), 443a (12 Aug., 1654) meaning
Ninth Report Appendix II, page 443,
column 1 (a letter dated 12 Aug. 1654,
referring to an event in 1645)

As already stated, the page-references in our Subject-Index do not lead to the Reports of the Commissioners but to the Inspectors' Reports. To his
description of the manuscripts in a collection, the
inspector usually prefixes a brief summary, which,
especially in the later Reports, is often helpful and
illuminating. We do not always give references to
mention of an item in the summary, but only to its
description or digest in the body of the Inspector's
Report. As for the Reports of the Commissioners,

19

these are of course important, and in our "List of Collections" we have included the numbers of these Reports. For instance, the description of the collection of the Marquess of Bath, in the Third Report, Appendix, pages 180-202, is introduced by the Commission in the Report proper, page xiii. Later these same manuscripts were calendared and published in a three-volume set, of which only Volumes I and II concern us. The Sixteenth and Seventeenth Reports of the Commission introduce these two volumes. In our Subject-Index there are no entries referring to Reports XVI and XVII, but in the "List of Collections" we give: "Bath, III, XVI, XVII, Vol. I, Vol. II," since all are important for study of the Bath manuscripts within the scope of this Guide.

We have tried to make the erratic seventeenth-century spelling of names of well-known persons, families and places conform to accepted usage, but little or no attempt has been made to clear up obscurities as to names or subject matter in the text. Doubtless many entries appear under quite the wrong headings and the compiler's digest of the inspector's record of the contents of a manuscript item may have gone far astray. An item from an early Report recorded as appearing in more than one collection or Report may actually be not the same item. Only the original manuscript can give the true meaning, especially if the notice of it is meagre, as is often true of the early folio Reports.

The question is, can the original manuscript be consulted? Some help toward an answer to this question is given by certain of the guides, listed as "Aids to the Use of the Reports," following this Introduction. In other respects, too, these works will take us further than does our Subject-Index. Titles in this list, which does not pretend to be exhaustive, have been annotated with special reference to the period of time, the subjects, and the particular Reports that are within the scope of this Guide; also to measures which the researcher can take to obtain access to the original manuscripts. Though individual manuscripts are rarely noted, to know that the bulk of a particular collection is still intact, and where it is kept, or where considerable groups of its manuscripts are to be consulted, is to make a start on this quest.

For names of persons, families and places the Commission's own Indexes are the chief reliance. References in these Indexes to volume only of a Report must be looked up in the index of the volume itself to find the page.

Names are only incidental in our Subject-Index, which is strictly a topical guide. It brings out under subject-headings some hundreds of items relating to English history between 1603 and 1660 on particular pages in the first nine Reports and in Reports supplementary to them. It is presented as a means of unearthing hidden materials and extending the area of research in that critical period of the history of

England.

AIDS TO THE USE OF THE REPORTS OF THE HISTORICAL MANUSCRIPTS COMMISSION

A Bibliography

Annotated with special reference to English history from 1603 to 1660 and to the availability of the original MSS. The term "Report" used herein refers to Reports of the Commissioners and Reports of the Inspectors as well.

General Guides

1. Roberts, Richard Arthur. The Reports of the Historical MSS. Commission. London, S.P.C.K.; New York, Macmillan, 1920. (Helps for students of history, no. 22)
By the Secretary of the Commission.
Treats briefly of the work of the Commission, of the nature and use of its two kinds of Reports, and of its "Guide to the Reports, Part I, Topographical." Surveys the contents of each Report, noting collections important for certain periods and for certain topics, such as "Virginia," "Travels," "Navy."

2. Ellis, Roger H. The Historical Manuscripts Commission, 1869-1969 (In Journal of the Society of Archivists, vol. II, no. 6 (October, 1962)
By the Secretary of the Commission.
Describes the work of the Commission under present

conditions and terms of reference, and carries on the story from R. A. Roberts' account.

3. Roberts, Richard Arthur. Concerning the Historical Manuscripts Commission. (In Royal Historical Society. Transactions, 3d ser., IV, 1910, p. 63-81)

Names several classes of papers likely to be found in family muniment rooms and the treatment that is given to each class by the Commission's Reports.

4. Historical Manuscripts Commission. Twenty-Second Report. London, H. M. Stationery Office, 1946.

Appendix I was the most complete key thus far to the structure and contents of the Reports. Groups the Commission's publications, each series together, instead of chronologically as in previous Reports. Lists the MS. collections treated in each Report, collection by collection, giving in some places a double title for a collection better known by name of place, for example, "Countess Cowper (Wrest Park MSS.)." Though the 22d Report is now out of print, this information is available, revised and with a fuller introductory note, in H. M. Stationery Office's Sectional List 17. (No. 7 on this list).

Appendix II, Archives of Corporate Bodies, is not within the scope of this Guide.

Appendix III, giving locations and ownership of privately-owned MS. collections upon which the Commission had reported since the beginning, has been superseded by Appendix III ("Location List") to the 24th Report. (No. 6 on this list)

Appendix IV is an index to the MS. collections reported on, giving in most cases the short title, the
original owner, and the original place of deposit,
with mention of subsidiary collections. It has not
yet (1963) been superseded and is still useful.

5. Historical Manuscripts Commission. Twenty-Third
Report, 1946-1959. London, H. M. Stationery Office,
1961.

Describes the Commission's revised policy and
extended program under the new Royal Warrant of
1959, and the closer association of the National
Register of Archives with the rest of the Commission's work. With emphasis rather on consultation
of original MSS., the present series of printed
calendars is to be gradually brought to a close; of
the series belonging to the field covered by this
Guide, four more volumes (XIX-XXII) of the Salisbury (Cecil) papers, two more (II-III) of the Sack-
ville (Knole) papers, and two more (V-VI) of the De
L'Isle and Dudley papers are planned. Most of the
Commission's work of inspection is now carried out
by the staff and helpers of the National Register of
Archives, in which their reports (in the form of
typescript lists) are placed. Summaries of these
reports (replacing the Summaries of Selected Reports formerly printed in the Bulletin of the National
Register of Archives) are to be printed in an

Appendix to future Reports to the Crown.

Appendix I. A full report by the Registrar on the work of the National Register of Archives from 1946 to 1959, describing inter alia how its reports are reproduced and circulated to record offices and libraries.

Appendix II. Contains summaries of all the separately numbered reports added to the National Register of Archives between September, 1957 and October, 1959, arranged by counties. Some of these reports relate to MS. collections already treated in the Commission's series of calendars.

6. Historical Manuscripts Commission. Twenty-Fourth Report, 1960-1962. London, H. M. Stationery Office, 1962.

Among announcements of volumes published or in progress are: De L'Isle and Dudley MSS. Vol. V, covering 1611 to 1626; the second part of the Index of Persons, covering Reports issued between 1911 and 1957; also volumes issued under the new Joint Publication Plan, by which the Commission publishes selected material prepared by Record Societies. This list includes the Letter Books of Sir Samuel Luke, 1644-45, of which one volume is described in the Eighth Report, Appendix III. A joint committee of the Commission and the British Records Association is preparing a List of Record Repositories in Great Britain, to replace that published by the British Records Association in 1956, now out of print. The series of printed Reports has been completely reproduced on microcards, which are held at the Commission's offices.

Appendices I and II continue those of the Twenty-Third Report.

Appendix III, "Location List." Shows, in alphabetical order, the MS. collections upon which the Commission has reported; the date and reference of the relevant Report; and, at the end of each entry, the present owner, custodian or place of deposit, as far as can be ascertained. References from alternate names of collections are included. This supersedes Appendix III of the 22d Report, in a more condensed and convenient form. It shows a marked advance since 1946 in the availability of the original manuscripts.

7. H. M. Stationery Office. Government publications. Sectional list no. 17. Publications of the Royal Commission on Historical Manuscripts.

In the issue revised to 30th June, 1961, is contained: List of publications. A. The Reports. Commissioners' Reports to the Crown. Inspectors' Reports to the Commissioners. (B) Other publications; Alphabetical list of manuscript collections upon which the Historical Manuscripts Commission has reported (under short titles); Chronological summary of Publications to 1957.

Revises and brings up to date the material in Appendix I of the Twenty-Second Report, with a fuller introduction.

8. University of London. Institute of Historical Research. Bulletin. London, New York, Toronto, Longmans.

Issued twice a year, May and November. The following sections in current issues frequently contain material bearing on the Historical Manuscripts Commission and the collections upon which it reports:

Historical Notes (formerly "Notes and News").

Mentions current work and publications of the Commission.

Historical Manuscripts. A. Accessions.

Formerly listed historical MSS. "which have reached a presumably permanent home in the custody of some public or corporate body." Now replaced by the National Register of Archives. Lists of Accessions to Repositories. Beginning in 1955 the Bulletin has listed only those MSS. which are incorporated into the collections of the British Museum, giving their numbering.

Historical Manuscripts. B. Migrations.

A select list of historical MSS. recently offered for sale by booksellers or auctioneers.

There is an index, mainly of personal and place-names, to sections A and B together, at the end of each volume of the Bulletin.

9. National Register of Archives. Bulletin, 1948 (-date) London, H.M. Stationery Office, 1948 (- date).

Some of the following may contain mention of MSS. already reported upon by the Historical Manuscripts Commission.

Nos. 2-5, 7 and 9 include Summaries of Selected Reports received. Since 1959 Summaries of all Reports received by the National Register of Archives have been given in Appendix I to current Reports of the Commission.

Nos. 10 - include brief descriptions of some important archive accumulations with which the Register has been specially concerned.

10. National Register of Archives. Lists of Accessions to Repositories, 1957 (- date) London, H.M. Stationery Office, 1958 (-date).

Takes the place of the Lists of Accessions in the Bulletin of the University of London Institute of Historical Research.

Lists covering accessions to Repositories in 1954 and 1955 were issued as special numbers, 6 and 8 of the Bulletin of the National Register of Archives.

An index is published periodically.

11. Historical Association.   County records.   By F.G.
    Emmison and Irvine Gray. London, Published for
    the Historical Association by George Philip and son,
    ltd., 1948. (Its Special series, S3)

    Describes the classes of source-material in Quarter
    Sessions records and other official archives of the
    English and Welsh counties.   Gives examples of
    topography and genealogy, also of local and national
    history in county records.

    Appendix I.   County records in print.

    Appendix II.   The County Record Office and the
    student.

    A condensed analysis of replies to a questionnaire
    on certain classes of records and facilities for their
    study in County Record Offices.

12. Read, Conyers, ed. Bibliography of British History,
    Tudor period, 1485-1603.   Issued under the direc-
    tion of the American Historical Association and the
    Royal Historical Society of Great Britain. Second
    edition.   Oxford, Clarendon Press, 1959.   I.
    General works covering the Tudor period. D. Source
    collections.   3. Historical MSS. Commission Re-
    ports.

    A list of collections which, though selected and
    noted for material on the Tudor period, includes a
    number containing items on the period 1603-1660.

It is preceded by a general account of the Reports
and guides to them; also of the National Register of
Archives. More recent publications of these are
listed in this Guide. Under "Sources" in particular
sections in the book are some references to the
Reports.

13. Davies, Godfrey, ed. Bibliography of British History, Stuart period, 1603-1714. Issued under the
direction of the Royal Historical Society and the
American Historical Association. Oxford, Clarendon
Press, 1928. Section I. English political and
constitutional history. 1. General and miscellaneous.
(a) Bibliographies, guides, sources.

Under this, nos. 1-178 include titles of guides to
the Reports, and names of collections, with brief
mention of important groups of papers therein. Under
particular topics, numbers here and there throughout
the book refer to particular Reports.

A second edition of this work, edited by Mary
Frear Keller, to be issued under the direction of
the American Historical Association and the Royal
Historical Society, is in progress (1963).

14. Pargellis, Stanley, ed. Bibliography of British His-
tory, the eighteenth century, 1714-1789. Issued
under the direction of the American Historical
Association and the Royal Historical Society of
Great Britain. Edited by Stanley Pargellis and D. J.
Medley. Oxford, Clarendon Press, 1951. Section

31

XVII. Historical Manuscripts Commission Reports.

Under this A. "Owners, recipients, and writers of letters and papers" lists some collections and paper which run over from the Stuart period.

15. Lomas, Mrs. Sophia Crawford (Williamson). The State papers of the early Stuarts and the Interregnum (Royal Historical Society. Transactions, new ser., XVI, 1902)

   Names collections important for the period 1603-1660 (p. 118-123, 131-132).

16. Davenport, Frances Gardiner. Materials for Engli diplomatic history, 1509-1783, calendared in the Reports of the Historical Manuscripts Commission, with references to similar materials in the British Museum. (Historical Manuscripts Commission. Eighteenth Report, 1917. Appendix II)

   A chronological list, giving page-references to the Reports, or to entire volumes or series of volumes which consist mainly of these materials. Relations with any particular country can be traced only by reading the list through, as there is no index.

17. Terry, Charles Sanford. An index to the papers relating to Scotland . . .in the Historical MSS. Commission's Reports (1870-1907). Glasgow, MacLehose, 1908.

   A descriptive portion notes materials that have been published by clubs and societies; gives some

page-references to the Reports. A subject-index,
mainly personal and place-names, refers to pages
in the descriptive portion, and has been republished
in the following:

18. Matheson, Cyril. A catalogue of the publications of
Scottish historical and kindred clubs and societies,
and of the papers relative to Scottish history issued
by H.M. Stationery Office, including the Reports
of the Royal Commission on Historical MSS., 1908-
1927. Aberdeen, Milne and Hutchinson, 1928.

19. Jameson, John Franklin. Guide to the items
relating to American history in the Reports of the
English Historical Manuscripts Commission and their
Appendixes. (American Historical Association.
Annual Report for the year 1898. Washington,
Government Printing Office, 1899, p. 611-708)

Covers the Reports through the Fifteenth, Appendix
IX, and the Salisbury (Cecil) MSS., vol. I-VI.
Limited to the United States and to colonies in the
area now the United States, also to Newfoundland,
Canada, Cuba, Puerto Rico and the Philippines.
General items: "America" and "Items relating to
individual colonies" are each listed in order of
date, with page-references to the Reports. An index
of persons refers to the pages in this work, which
forms Appendix III of the Third Annual Report of
the (American) Historical Manuscripts Commission.

20. Historical Manuscripts Commission. A guide to
the Reports on collections of manuscripts . . .
issued by the Royal Commissioners for Historical
Manuscripts (1870-1911). Part I, Topographical
(edited by R. A. Roberts). London, H. M. Stationery
Office, 1914. (Parliament. Papers by command,
Cd. 7594)

Out of print. An index of place-names, usually
entered under the modern forms, but with variants
added as found in the Reports. A composite index
made up from the indexes in the Reports themselves, but giving references to volumes only, not
to pages, e.g., "2d R.," "Bath II." For page-
references we must turn to the index of the Report
itself.

21. Historical Manuscripts Commission. Guide to the
Reports of the Royal Commission on Historical
Manuscripts, Part II, Index of Persons: 1870-1911
(edited by Francis Bickley). London, H. M. Stationery Office, 1935-38. 2 volumes, of which vol.
2 is out of print; 1911-1957 (edited by A. L. S. Hall)
is in the press (1963)

A composite index like Part I, with references to
volumes only.

SUBJECT-INDEX

A Topical Guide to Materials on English History,
1603-1660, in collections of manuscripts represented
in Reports I to IX and subsequent Reports on these
collections.

Page-references to the Reports are given as in the
following examples:

> IX(2), 370a, b meaning Ninth Report,
> Appendix II, page 370, column 1 and
> column 2.

> Bath MSS., Vol. II, 57* meaning Calendar
> of the Manuscripts of the Marquis of Bath,
> Vol. II, page 57.

An asterisk means that the Report gives the contents
of the manuscript item with a fair degree of fullness.

The semicolon after a group of words in an index-
entry is a device to mark the termination of the main
head. What follows, either on the same line or indented below, is a sub-head.

Abatements upon marriage of Princess Elizabeth,
    1613,   III, 204a (no. 18) ; IV, 352b

Accounts (receipts and expenses) — Private;

17th cent. (early),	VI, 313a
1620— , 1629,	III, 292b
1656,	VI, 420b
Sir W. Cavendish, and others, to 1660,	III, 44a
of John Smith of Nibley (?), 1601-1640,	V, 360a

of Earl of Northumberland; 1602-1629,

                                      VI, 228b-231a

—; temp. Jac. 1,   V, 354b

—; 1604(?), for New Year's gifts
  and for portage of money,   III, 52b

—; 1616, Lord Percy created Knight
  of the Bath,   III, 63b

of Sir T. Edmondes, 1608-1620,   VII, 592a

of Francis, Earl of Cumberland,
  1614-1635,   III, 41b

of Earl of Northampton, 1616, 1623,

                                V, 409b, 410b

of the Scudamores, 1635-1643,	VII, 692b
of Sir R. Graham, 1640-1641,	VI, 330a
of Sir Fr. Throckmorton, 1643-1650,	III, 257b

of Lord Broghill, 1646,

                    Egmont MSS., Vol. I, 327*

of Sir P. Leycestre, 1648-1678,   I, 49b

Accounts (receipts and expenses) — Public (cont.);

during progresses, etc., 1615-1622,

III, 264b, 265a

for debts of Royal Wardrobe, 1622-
1635,   VII, 224b

for embassies of Lord Feilding, temp.
Car. 1,   VI, 287b; VII, 223b

for Hampton Court, 1632,   VI, 323a

of N. Hallows of Derby, "for the
Commonwealth," 1642-1645,   IX(2), 392a

for King's children, 1647-   ,   VI, 316b

for goods of Charles I (after 1651),   IX(2), 444b*

for embassy to Sweden, 1653-1654,   III, 190a

of Protectorate, 1654, 1659,   VIII(1), 98a

of constable, at Wirksworth, 1655,   IX(2), 395b

of Exchequer, 1656-1658,   VIII(1), 94b-95a*

of surveyor of shire hall, co. Derby,
1657,   IX(2), 395b

of profits of Court of Common Pleas,   III, 191b

See also: Army and militia; Colonies;
Finance, public; Horses; Household,
Royal; Naval and maritime affairs;
Prices; Revenue; Stables, Royal.

Acre, English, extent and yield of, compared
with French, 1620(?),   III, 64b

Admiralty, Court of; records, 1307-1670,   V, 259b

commissions, etc., in, temp. Car.1,   I, 34a, 43b

practise in, 1625,   I, 43b

Admiralty, Court of (cont.); civilians as judges
of, VII, 432b
law suits of Spanish ambassador in, V, 411a
no prohibition on suits commenced in,
1632, VII, 433a
certification of, relating to fishing
craft, 1632, V, 413a

Advance of Money, Committee for; see:
Haberdashers' Hall Committee.

Agriculture; prices of products of, 1601-
1608, IV, 414a*
bill for garden seeds, 1612, IV, 343a
prices of oats and hay, 1637, VI, 231b
lists of farmers' apprentices,
Lincolnshire, 1618, XII (4), 455
extent and yield of English and French
acre, 1620(?), III, 64b
correspondence of Abel Barker as
farmer and landholder, 1642-1660,
V, 387b-398a, passim*
amounts of corn threshed at (Berw), 1646
and 1647, V, 421b
invention for cultivating without oxen or
horses, I, 34a
See also: Inclosures; Landed estates.

Aids, feudal; at knighting of Prince Henry, 1609,
III, 196b and Bath MSS., Vol. II, 57*; V, 408a, b; VI,
229a
at marriage of Princess Elizabeth,

40

Aids, feudal; at marriage of Princess Elizabeth (cont.)
    1613,   II, 86a; XII (4), 440

Alehouses; 1603,   IX (2), 370a, b (no. 49, 50)
   licensing and regulation of; 1603,   III, 52b
   — ; 1608,   IV, 331a; XII (4), 410
   — ; temp. Jac. 1 - Car. 1,
        VII, 668b, 682a; IX (2), 370a, b (no. 49, 50)
   poacher forbidden to keep, 1624,   IX (2), 427a
   not to serve flesh in Lent, 1626, 1631,
                      V, 401b, 402a

Ales and revels, regulation of, 1632-1633,   III, 286a

Algerines; see: Pirates.

Alienation of Crown lands; see: Crown lands.

Alienations, Office of Composition for, temp.
   Jac. 1,   III, 214a

Aliens; see: Foreigners in England.

Almshouse, Statutes of Somerton, 1625,   VII, 593b

Almsmen, Lord Northampton's almsmen's
   clothing, etc., 1614,   V, 409

Alnage, patent for selling payments for,
   1628(?),   III, 286b

Alnagers of cloth, temp. Jac. 1,   III, 56a, 59a

Alum Commissioners, 1620(?),   II, 58a

Alum works, threatened suspension of,
   1644,   IX (2), 436b (9 Dec.)

Ambassadors and envoys; see: Foreign relations.

Amboina massacre, 1623,   III, 190b

Amusements; expenses for,
        Rutland MSS., Vol. IV, 447-541, passim*
Northumberland's expenses for,
  1603-1615,   VI, 228b-231a, passim
articles and arrangements for a raffle,
  1612,   III, 196b and Bath MSS., Vol. II, 61-62*
masque at marriage of princess, 1613,   II, 281b
presents at Mayor's feast, Stafford, 1622,

                         IV, 327b
regulation of ales and revels, 1632-1633, II, 286a
refreshment boats on the Thames, 1636, III, 191b
See also: Alehouses; Plays and players;
  Sports and games.

Anagrams and epigrams, on Gondomar,
  James I, and others,   IX(2), 375b

Animals, domestic; prices of livestock;
  1601-1608,   IV, 414a*
  —; 1618,   V, 417b
See also: Cattle; Dogs; Horses;
  Sheep.

Annuities; to Princess Elizabeth, from imposts
  on tobacco, 1637,   I, 34b
  to Queen, from customs, 1639,   V, 313a-b
  Northumberland's allowances to
    members of his family, 1606-1615,

                VI, 229a-231a, passim

Annuities; (cont.)

    to F. Babington from Earl of Shrewsbury,
      1609,   VI, 449b
    to Sir George and Sir Robert More
      in consideration of resignation, 1627,   VII, 676b
    See also: Pensions.

Apothecaries;   Rutland MSS., Vol. IV, 454, 464, 501*
    Queen Anne's apothecary, 1604,   II, 79a
    fees to, 1618,   IX(2), 425b (1 Oct.)
    payment to, for medicines delivered to
      sick prisoners in the Tower, 1617,   VII, 673b
    drugs to be purchased from, 1647   V, 389a
    Charles I's apothecary, payment to,
      1649,   III, 266a

Apprentices; terms for, 1656,   II, 64a*
    list of farmers' apprentices, Lincolnshire,
      1618,   XII(4), 455
    to wear caps, not hats, 1620,   IX(2), 389a
    to be prevented at London from taking
      service for Ireland, 1641(42),   V, 350a

Arches, Court of; see: Court of Arches.

Armor;   II, 48b; IV, 334a
    assessment for, Kelling Hall, 1605,   VI, 361b
    barons exempt from "showing of horse
      and armor,"   III, 43a
    rated on clergy, 1612,   II, 86a
    ironmonger's bill for leathering, 1660,
                      IX(2), 396a*

Armory, accounts of Master of, 1601-1610,

VII, 670a

Arms; payment for, 1616,   IV, 337a

    provided for service in Ireland, 1608,   VII, 669a

    deficiency of arms and ammunition, 1625   III, 40a

    list of R. Verney's, 1659,   VII, 461b

    to be made at Sheffield, 1638,   III, 40b*

    illegally possessed; 1612,   II, 86a

    —; in Worcestershire, 1654,   II, 36b

    permission to carry, 1659,   III, 293a

    See also: Civil Wars—Armies.

Army and militia—General; project,   IX(2), 378a

    orders and laws by the Lord Marshal,

    temp. Jac. 1,   VI, 328b

    strength of trained bands of Kent,

    1621,   Finch MSS., Vol. I, 42-43*

    training instructions for militia of Derby,

    1624,   IX(2), 389b

    muster-roll and maintenance of trained

    bands, Buckinghamshire, 1624,   VIII(3), 32a

    papers relating to, temp. Car. 1,   I, 51a

    estimates, etc., for, 1640-1641(?),   III, 84b

    in Surrey, June, August, 1642,   VII, 677b

    proposition concerning, answered by

    King, 9 Oct., (1648),   V, 313b

    accounts of J. Sharp for Gen. Fairfax,

    1650, 1653-1657,   VIII(1), 637b (no. 25)

    members of General Council of Army and Navy

    in England, Scotland and Ireland, 1659,

Army and militia—General (cont.);

VIII(3), 6b(no. 38)

commission of Monck for holding court
martial, 27 Mar., 1660,   V, 361a
See also: Bishops' War(s); Civil Wars,
1642-1651—Armies; Garrisons; Impressment;
Ireland— Rebellion of 1641 and Civil War;
Ordnance.

Army and militia—Assessments and charges; 25
soldiers for Ireland from co. Leicester,
22 Nov., 1616,   IX(2), 425a
rating of manors and lands, 1625,   III, 40a
objections to, 1627,   III, 40a
persons in Lacock refusing to pay,
1630(?),   III, 71a
Order in Council defining who is chargeable
for light horse or a lance, 1638,   V, 413a
in Worcestershire, 1647-1654,   I, 54b, 55a
on Gallow, Norfolk, 1651,   XI(7), 103-104
on Menai, 1653,   V, 422a
contribution from Penrose, 1654,   VII, 689a
charges for, 1654, 1659,   VIII(1), 98a
Exchequer payment for forces in
England and at Dunkirk and Mardike,
1657-1658,   VIII(1), 94b-95a*
a horse or Ł 10 required from
R. Verney, 1659,   VII, 461b
charge of Ł 10 for horse and arms,
1659,   Finch MSS., Vol. I, 78*

Army and militia—Musters; (cont.)

—; to Archbishop of Canterbury, 1608, V, 311b

official letters to Earl of Devonshire,
1625, 1626, III, 42b

ordered by Warwick, 1634, VII, 549a

co. Derby; 1619, XII(4), 455

—; 1621, XII(4), 460

—; 1630, IX(2), 389b

co. Huntington, Sept., 1638, VIII(2), 55a

Hillington, co. Norfolk, 1639, III, 247b

co. Lincoln, 1618, XII(4), 454

London, hamlets pertaining to the
Tower, VIII(1), 88a

Prees, co. Salop, 1633 and 1634, III, 258b

co. Stafford (?), 1621, IV, 334a

co. Stafford, 1642, V, 141b

Stoughton, 1626, VIII(2), 50a

Surrey, muster-master of, 1615,
1625, VII, 671b, 675b, 676a

Sussex, 1640(?), III, 83b

Tallabollion and Tindaethwy,
1602-1644, V, 416a-420b, passim

Wilts, muster book of, 1637, III, 120b

Winchelsea, muster roll of, 1634, II, 92a

for war on Continent, 1624, II, 87b

See also: Array, Commissioners of.

Army and militia—Officers; pay for officers of
troop of horse, temp. Car. 1(?),

IX(2), 369b (no. 6)

Army and militia—Officers; (cont.)

Fairfax to be colonel of 1000 trained-band
soldiers in West Riding, 21 June, 1641,

IX(2), 432b

purchase of advancement, 1647,   VII, 438a-b*

officers' commissions, 1659, 1660,

VIII(3), 6b (no. 39-41)

Army and militia—Supplies and pay; payment for
victualling and transportation to Vlissinghen
of soldiers heretofore in pay at Carlisle,
1604,   VI, 471b

Privy Council letter concerning, 1624,   I, 41a

cost of supply per month, temp.
Car. 1(?),   IX(2), 369b (no. 6)

reluctance of persons to pay salaries of
soldiers, 1628,   VII, 677a

for Guernsey and Jersey, Jan., 1628(29), III, 70b

pay for "auncient-bearer (ensign-bearer)
under Captaine Thomas Powell," 1629, V, 412b

pay of officers, 1629,   VII, 545b

arrears to be paid to officers, 1637,

IX(2), 431a (5 June)

plate coined for soldiers' pay, 1641, VII, 435a-b

Sir R. (i.e. Sir P.) Perceval's defense
in parliament of his conduct as
Commissary General of Victual in
Ireland, 1647,   VII, 233b

pay for impressed men, 1651,

IX(2), 441b (4 June)*

48

Army and militia—Troops; transport of Morton's
　　troops to Scotland from Surrey (Council
　　letter), 1628,　　　　　　　　　　　VII, 677a
　　for service of King of Sweden (1631),　IX(2), 370b
　　cuirassier to be at charges of J. Smith,　V, 345b
　　artillery of Marquis Hamilton, Feb.,
　　　1639 (40),　　　　　　　　　　　　　III, 81a
　　unpaid soldiers stealing near Ripon
　　　(1641),　　　　　　　　　　　　　VII, 435a, b*
　　Hugh Peters suggests medals for soldiers,
　　　1645,　　　　　　　　　　　　　　IX(2), 438a
　　soldiers to be outfitted by J. Gell at
　　　Hopton, 1651,　　　　　　　　　　IX, (2) 395a
　　appointment of T. Pury to command
　　　foot at Gloucester, 1659,　　　　　V, 361a
　　levy of; in Surrey, temp. Jac. 1,
　　　Car. 1,　　　　　　　　　VII, 669a, 675b, 678b
　　—; 1613-1622,　　　　　　　　　　IV, 331a
　　—; volunteers, 1624,　　　　　　　XII(4), 470
　　—; recruits, not of the trained bands,
　　　from Hundred of Martinsley, co. Rutland,
　　　for service abroad, 1625,　　　　V, 401b
　　—; in Wilts, 1638(?),　　　　　　III, 76a
　　—; for Cromwell, 1654-1655,　　　IX(2), 395b
　　—; under Col. Legh, 1659,　　　　III, 269a
　　—; for service in Ireland; from
　　　Derbyshire, 1607,　　　XII(4), 407, 408, 410
　　—; —; from Staffordshire, 1616,　　IV, 343b
　　quartering of; Mar., 1627(28),　　III, 278a

Army and militia—Troops; (cont.)

—; at Farnham, Surrey (Council letter),
1628,   VII, 677a

—; at Cottingham, co. York, Jan., 1640,
(41),   III, 83b

—; protection from, 1659,   III, 293a

sick or disabled,   V, 403b*; VI, 336a

foot; list of 100 footmen levied in Surrey,
1627,   VII, 676b

—; for service of Sweden, 1631,   III, 190b-191a

—; to be raised in Sussex, 1640(?),   III, 83b

horse; list of, Staffordshire, 1634,   II, 48b

—; exercises, 1635,   VII, 530b

—; Order in Council stating number
of and charges for horse per county,
1638,   V, 413a

—; agreement to complete troops of,
Nov., 1640,   III, 83a

—; list and pay of officers of dragoons,
Cumberland(?), Feb., 1639 (40),   III, 81a

Army Plot, First, 1641,
       V, 413b; Egmont MSS., Vol. I, 134*

Array, Commissioners of; their letters to
Earl of Derby, 1640 and 1641,   I, 47a

in Worcestershire; royal instructions to,
June (1642),   II, 36b

—; flight of, Aug., 1644,   IV, 270a

See also: Army and militia—Musters.

Art; collections of, 1635, VI, 279b
  art objects for a raffle,
    1612, III, 196b and Bath MSS., Vol. II, 61-62*
  tapestries and statues belonging to
    Charles I, IX(2), 444b*
  See also: Pictures.

Assemblies, "disorderly," near parish church,
  Eskiviog, 1643, V, 420a

Assessments, rates; for armor, Kelling Hall,
  1605, VI, 361b
  on Martinsley Hundred for "reparation" of
    St. Paul's, 1633, V, 402a
  quarter pay in Worcestershire, 1647-
    1654, I, 55a
  monthly tax in North Wales, V, 422a
  in places in Essex, 1651-1700, VII, 593b
  in Norfolk, 1651, III, 272b
  on lands in Norfolk, 1610-1611, VIII(3), 30b(no. 7)
  in Menai, for armies and navies, V, 422a
  in Penrose, 1653, 1654, VII, 689a
  in Cuckfield, Sussex, 1654, VII, 678b
  in co. Flint for disbanding forces,
    1660, VI, 425a
  on land of Lady Rivers, 1643, VII, 549b
  of Sir J. Isham (period of Commonwealth), III, 254a
  of T. Parmenter an informer, 1656.
               Lothian Mss., p. 88*
  See also: Army and militia— Assessments and
    charges; Civil Wars— Finance— Parliamentary;

Assessments, rates; See also: (cont.);

Civil Wars— Finance— Royalist; Subsidies; Taxation.

Assizes; fees taken by judges at,   III, 192b

    indictments and offenders at,

      Derbyshire, 1616,   XII (4), 449*

    duties of constables at, temp. Jac. 1 or

      Car. 1,   IX (2), 370b (no. 52, 54)

    justices of, 1605,   VII, 526b

    duties of High Sheriff at, 1647,   V, 390a-b, 397a

    arrangements for, Rutland, July, 1647,   V, 397a

    See also: Juries.

Associated Counties, Eastern; see: Eastern

    Association.

Assurance, Office of, in London, 1634,   I, 34b

Baize, counterfeiting of seals for, 1632,   III, 71a-b

Bakehouse, Royal, accounts of, temp. Jac. 1

    or Car. 1,   VII, 592a-b*

Bankrupt, Commissions of, temp. Car. 1,   I, 34a

Baronage, Lord Spencer's fees for, 1603,   II, 19b*

Baronetcies, payments for, 1632,   II, 47a-b*

    proposed abolition of, (temp. Jac. 1),

      VI, 312a; IX (2), 369b (no. 13)

    opinion of "Garter and others" concerning,

      10 Jac. 1,   VI, 459b

    warrants for patents of, temp. Car. 1,   I, 34b

Baronets; 1611, 1612,   XII (4), 431, 434*

    list of, 1611,   XII (4), 432

Benevolences and loans to the King (cont.);

    privy seals; temp. Jac. 1,

        III, 38b, 39b, 40a, 120a; VII, 668a; IX (2), 366a (no. 80)

—; calendar of, in Cheshire, 1625,   I, 46b

gentry to lend money, 1625,   III, 42b

for Palatine war, 1622,   VI, 461a

security to Lord Keeper Coventry for

    loan, (1640),   IV, 229a

opinions on the proposed forced loan from

    London, 5 May, 1640,   III, 81b

warrant of Charles I for loan of ₤20,

    1643,   VIII (3), 6b, 7a

asked for, from;

—; co. Derby, 1614, 1622, 1622 (23),

    1626,   XII (4), 442, 464, 469, 478

—; Surrey, temp. Jac. 1, Car. 1,

           VII, 670a, b, 675a, 678b

—; Oxfordshire, 1625,   V, 411b

—; Earl of Hertford, 1627,   III, 282b

—; T. Saunders, 1642,   III, 265b

—; Sir J. Isham, 1642,   III, 254a

contributed by;

—; J. Arcel, 1607,   III, 264b

—; W. Prade, 1611,   IV, 405a

—; G. Austen, 1614,   VII, 671a

—; J. Prade, (n. d.),   II, 99a

—; J. Wilson, 1625,   V, 304b

—; Sir P. Mutton, 1626,   III, 258a

—; T. Tickell, 1636,   VIII (1), 211a

Benevolences and loans to the King; contributed
  by (cont.);
  —; the Bishop of Worcester, 1642,   II, 78b

Bible, Codex Alexandrinus, 1653,   V, 314a

Bible, Polyglot; English scholars engaged
    on, 1653,   Bath MSS., Vol. II, 111*
  printing of, (n. d.),   V, 313b, 314b

Bills; see: Accounts (receipts and expenses) —Private.

Biographical notes ("Characters") and
  epigrams,   VII, 244a-b; IX (2), 362a (no. 436), 375b

Bishops; consecration of, etc., 1621,   II, 60a
  speech on innovations by, Feb. 1640 (41),   III, 83b
  patents for creation of, and congés d'élire,
    temp. Car. 1,   I, 34a
  petition against Bishop of Oxford, 1622,   V, 410a
  accusations against Bishop of Bangor,
                              V, 417b-418a*
  instructions of Archbishop Abbott to bishops
    of Province of Canterbury, (n. d.),   V, 408b;
                              IX (2), 370a (no. 30)
  extortion of fees charged to Bishop of
    Exeter, 1628,   IX (2), 428b (21 Sept.)
  dispute of jurisdiction between Bishop of
    Bangor and his chancellor,   V, 412b
  suspension of Bishop of Lincoln (letter of
    Laud), 1637,   VIII (1), 209b*

Bishops' Wars, 1639-1640; charges raised and

Boats, refreshment, on the Thames, 1636,   III, 191b

Books; expenses for;

      Rutland MSS., Vol. IV, 444-521, passim*

—; by Northumberland,   VI, 229a-231a

—; by J. Perceval at Cambridge,

  1647,   Egmont MSS., Vol. I, 474-475*

lists and catalogues of; at Mostyn

  libraries,   IV, 347b, 351a, 352b, 354a

—; and authors (including English history),

          VIII(3), 17a (no. 3, 12, 14)

—; sent to Syon from the Tower by

  Northumberland, 1614,   VI, 231b

heretical, in possession of Digby in Spain,

  1611,   VIII(1), 213a*

imported by Arundell, Jan., 1636(37),

          VIII(1), 554a*

presented to University of Oxford; 1640, III, 189a

—; by J. Selden,   V, 312b; VI, 420b

S. D'Ewes to J. Selden on lexicons, etc.,

  1649,   V, 312b

seditious pamphlet by Bedford, 1629(?),   VI, 459a

Sir T. Bodley's "Cogitata et Visa," etc., VI, 350a

Sir T. Browne's "Religio Medici," 1642,

          IX(2), 371a (no. 688)

William Burton's "Graecae Linguae Historia,"

  1656,   V, 312b

"Defensio Regia pro Carolo Primo"

  suppressed in Holland, 1650,   V, 314a

Exchequer pays for printing maps for

Books (cont.);

Church of England; (cont.);
    1611,   VIII(1), 213a-b*
    See also: Clergy; Protestantism.

Churches; vessels, vestments, etc.,
      concealed by a recusant, 1617,   VII, 543b
    storing of altar furniture, 1621,   V, 410a
    removing "scandalous" pictures from,
      1642,   V, 350b
    regulation of, by Parliamentary Committee
      of Dorset, 1646-1650,   VIII(1), 210b
    foreign; in London, 1634,   III, 212a
    —; French church in Somerset chapel,   V, 314a
    "disorderly assemblies"; near church of
      Eskiviog, 1643,   V, 420a (no. A132)
    —; at St. Saviour's, Southwark, 1641,   VII, 686a
    rights to seats, burial places, etc.;
      1631,   VI, 424a
    —; at Eskiviog, 1641, 1642,   V, 419b-420a*
    —; at Mold,   VI, 423b, 424a
    —; at Ruthlan, 1621,   VI, 423b-424a
    —; at Wrexham, 1659,   VI, 425a
    repair of; Bangor Cathedral, 1636,   V, 419a
    —; St. Paul's, London,
                  II, 88a; III, 191a, 211b-212a;
         V, 345b, 402a; VI, 472a; Lothian MSS., p. 84*
    —; Christ Church, Norwich, 1633,   XI(7), 97*
    —; Selby Church, 1623,   II, 18a
    Canterbury Cathedral Statutes, 1636,
                      VIII(3), 31a (no. 28)

Churches (cont.);

OUTLINE FOR CIVIL WARS, 1642-1651

General history (covering more than two
years, or undated)

History by place (covering more than two
years, or undated)

Finance

  Parliamentary

    General

    Assessments, etc.

  Royalist

Negotiations and foreign relations

Captivity of Charles I

Armies

  In general or not specified

  Parliamentary

    In general

    Troops

    Supplies and pay

  Royalist

Naval affairs (not connected with military
operations)

History by year (covering two years or
less)

  1642

  1642-1643

  1643

  1643-1644

1644

1644-1645

1645

1645-1646

1646

1647

1648

1648-1649

1649

1650

1651

Dates of the MSS. (e.g. letters) are not necessarily
the dates of the events referred to. No "See also"
references are given to "Diaries, journals and memoirs,
"Letters (collections), "Letters of news," of this period,
though additional material on the Civil Wars will almost
surely be found in manuscript items for which there
are entries under these headings. Any diaries or
letters concerned mainly with the Civil Wars are
referred to under the headings listed in the above out-
line.

Civil Wars, 1642-1651—General history (covering
    more than two years, or undated); chronology of
    events in England and Wales, 1640-1656, IV, 356b
    occurrences,   VI, 449a
    "Epitome,"   VIII(3), 16a
    operations of forces under Sir J. Gell,

Civil Wars, 1642-1651—General history (covering more
 than two years, or undated) (cont.);
 1624-1644, IX(2),387a-388a*
 Fairfax's memorials, 1642-1644, VI, 465b-466a
 narrative of Capt. J. Hodgson, 1642-
 1665, III,121b
 notices of events by Sir N. Lechmere,
 V, 299a-300a
 newsletters; Aug., 1642-July, 1640
 (1644?), II, 47b-48a
 —; of F. Godolphin, 1642-1645 (?), II, 99a
 extracts from newspapers, 1643-1657,
 VIII(3), 12a (no. 23)
 minutes of proceedings of Parliamentary
 Committee for Dorset, 1646-1650, VIII(1), 210b
 search for compromising papers of
 W. Wilson by Cromwell's soldiers, V, 305a
 letter from J. Crofts in Royalist forces
 near Oxford, IX(2), 370a (no. 39)
 denial of charges by King's commissioners,
 1642(?), III, 85b*
 Earl of Northumberland's losses in the
 war, III, 86b
 letters and papers of; Elizabeth, countess of
 Denbigh, IV, 260b-261b*
 —; Susan, countess of Denbigh, IV, 258b-260b*
 —; Sir T. Barrington, of Committee for
 Essex, 1642-1644,
 VII, 549b-570a, 577a-578a, passim*

Civil Wars, 1642-1651—General history (covering more
   than two years, or undated); letters and papers of (co
   —; Edward, Lord Mandeville (afterwards
   2d Earl of Manchester), 1642-1646,

                             VIII(2), 59-63*

   —; Lieut.-Col. J. Baines, 1642-1647,

                             VII, 686a-687b

   —; Verney family, 1642-1649,   VII, 439a-457a*

   —; Charles I and other leaders of both
   sides, 1642-1651,   IX(2), 433b-441b*

   —; Sir J. Gell and Committee of Derby,
   1642-1651,   IX(2), 391a-395a*

   —; Abel Barker and family, of Hambleton,
   co. Rutland, 1642-1660,   V, 387-398

   —; Basil, 2d Earl of Denbigh, 1643-
   1645,   IV, 262a-276a*

See also: Parliamentary affairs; Parliamentary
   proceedings.

Civil Wars, 1642-1651—History by place (covering
   more than two years, or undated); Anglesey,
   resolutions, etc., of gentry,   V, 420b-421a*

Bedfordshire, papers of Committee
   for,   VIII(1), 2b-11a, passim*

Belvoir Castle, 1647-1649,   XII(5), 3-4, 6*

Cheshire, T. Malbon's account of, V, 333a, 339a

Chester, 1642-1650,   V, 344a-b

Chirk Castle,   II, 73b

papers of Sir J. Gell and Committee of
   Derby, 1642-1651,   IX(2), 391a-395a*

Civil Wars, 1642-1651—History by place (covering
    more than two years, or undated) (cont.);
   minutes of proceedings of Parliamentary
    Committee for Dorset, 1646-1650,   VIII(1), 210b
   papers of Sir T. Barrington, of Committee for
    Essex, 1642-1644,

               VII, 549b-570a, 577a-578a, passim*

   Gloucestershire, letters and papers of J. Smith
    of Nibley, 1642-1643,   V, 345b-347a
   Hitchin (Herts), assault against, (n.d.), VII, 576a
   Ireland; see: Ireland, Rebellion of 1641 and
    Civil War.
   Lathom House, two sieges,   V, 333a, 339a
   Newport Pagnell, contributions of
    Bedfordshire to defense of,
    1644-1646,   VIII(1), 3a-10b, passim
   Sherborne House,   III, 191b
   Wales; 1642-1651,   IV, 356b
   —; 1644-1646,   II, 86b-87a
   Worcestershire, letters of Lyttleton
    family in,   II, 36a-b
   Yorkshire (action near Cottingham,
    Newland, Holderness),   VII, 575b*
   See also: Civil Wars, 1642-1651—History by
    year; Eastern Association.

Civil Wars, 1642-1651—Finance— Parliamentary—
   General; further exactions from recusants
   petitioned for,   IV, 273b
   goods and money raised in Walsall, etc.,

Civil Wars, 1642-1651—Armies—Parliamentary—In
  general (cont.);
  officers and soldiers; send petition to Sir T.
  Fairfax, 1648(?),   III, 87a
  —; their demands,   V, 414a
  officers; their names, colors and arms,
  1642-1645,   II, 365b
  —; list of, under command of Sir T.
  Fairfax,   VI, 362b

Civil Wars, 1642-1651—Armies—Parliamentary—
  Troops; their conduct, Apr., 1644,
                            Denbigh MSS., Vol. V, 76*
  impressment; constables unable to carry
  out, (1643)   VII, 577b
  —; and inspection, etc., Sept., 1644,
                                    XI(7), 101-102*
  levy of foot in Yorkshire, 1645,   VI, 362a
  Denbigh's quota, 1650, Denbigh MSS., Vol. V, 81*
  their quartering and billeting;   IV, 272a-b
  —; in Eastern Association, forbidden to
  Fairfax's army, Mar., 1646(47),   IV, 274a
  —; in Rutland, 1646, 1649,
                        V, 390a, 392a*, 397a; V, 403b*
  —; in Somerset (troops bound for Ireland),
  1647,   Egmont MSS., Vol. I, 403*
  —; in Wressell, 1648,   III, 86b, 87a
  for Ireland; 1647,   IV, 294a
  —; 1649,   I, 55b
  regiment of foot under Sir J. Gell,

Civil Wars, 1642-1651—Armies—Parliamentary—
   Troops (cont.);
   1642-1644,   IX(2), 387a-388a*

Civil Wars, 1642-1651—Armies—Parliamentary—
   Supplies and pay; 1644,   Vol. V, 77-79*
to be advanced by Receiver-General of
   Revenue, 1647,   VI, 224a
pay of soldiers,
           VI, 472b; IX(2), 395a (22 Feb., 1650)*
papers of Lieut. Col. J. Baines, including
   regimental accounts, 1642-1647,   VII, 686a-687b
arms and gunpowder; Essex, 1642, 1643,
                       VII, 577a, b*
—; for Tallabollion militia, 1645,   V, 420b
order by Fairfax to restore wood taken
   by soldiers, 1648,   V, 361a
levy on private persons for horse and pay
   for service in Scotland, 1650,   VIII(1), 637b
charges of foot soldiers against Committee
   of Parliament allowed, 1651,   VII, 687a
horses;   V, 298a; VI, 472b; VII, 577b
—; plundered by King's army,
   1645,   VIII(1), 9a (5 Sept., 1645)
—; requisitions of fodder, beds and,
   1644,   V, 402b, 403a
—; for Eastern Association, 1643-1645,
                      VIII(2), 60a

Civil Wars, 1642-1651—Armies—Royalist; 1643-
   1644,   IV, 263, 266, passim*

Civil Wars, 1642-1651—Naval affairs (not connected
    with military operations) (cont.);

    1648,   IX(2), 439b-440a*
    seizures at sea;   II, 161-165, passim*
    —; 1645, 1646,   Egmont MSS., Vol. I, 251, 278*

Civil Wars, 1642-1651—History by year (covering two
    years or less)—1642; letters of John Hampden
    and others,   VIII(3), 6a
    newsletters; 6, 17 June,   V, 141a, b*
    —; Oct.,   V, 142b; VII, 530b-531a*
    —; 13 Dec.,   V, 142a*
    Berkeley Castle, arrangements for defense
    of, 23 Sept.,   V, 333a, 356a
    Brentford, battle at, 15 Nov.,
                        Egmont MSS., Vol. I, 182
    Chester, activities in, June-Aug.,   V, 350b-352b
    Edgehill, Battle of,   V, 143b, 414a (no. 732)
    Essex; tumults in, Aug.,   IV, 262b
    —; declaration of loyalty of,   VII, 577b*
    —; recruiting in Braintree and Bocking,
                                    VII, 576a
    Hull, siege of,   VI, 362b
    Manchester, diary of siege of, Sept.,   V, 142a-b
    Monmouth, fear caused by army in,
    Oct.,   VII, 689a*
    Norfolk; foreign forces off coast of,
    Dec.,   III, 247b
    —; Cromwell orders troops raised in,
    20 Mar.,   IX(2), 367b

Civil Wars, 1642-1651—History by year (covering
    two years or less) — 1642 (cont.);

Portsmouth reduced, Sept.,   VIII(2), 59a (no. 506)

Surrey, military forces in, Oct.,   VII, 677b

Warwick, Royalist situation in, Aug.,   II, 36b*

Worcester, orders of Association of North-
    west Part of, (1642?),   II, 48b

York, gentry attending King at,   III, 294b; IV, 408b

Civil Wars, 1642-1651—History by year (covering two
    years or less) —1642-1643; letters and papers of
    John Smith of Nibley,   V, 346a

Civil Wars, 1642-1651—History by year (covering two
    years or less) —1643; newsletter; 19 Mar.,
                             V, 143b

—; 21 May,   VIII(2), 59b

—; 9 Dec.,   VI, 335b

letter of R. Hopton, 30 Oct.,   I, 58a

report by Sir R. Lloyd of operations in
    Northwest, (25 Dec.),   III, 259a

Aylesbury, Buckinghamshire forces
    ordered to,   III, 276a*

Berkeley Castle, surrender of, Feb.,
                            V, 333a, 356a-b

Chester; orders from Col. Davies to march,
    Dec.,   III, 259a

—; Sir A. Shipman at,   IV, 263a

Chirk Castle, orders of King for defense
    of, Dec.,   III, 259a

Civil Wars, 1642-1651—History by year (covering two
    years or less)—1644 (cont.);

  to Prince Rupert,   I, 47a

correspondence of Sir S. Luke, at
  Newport Pagnell,   VIII(3), 12b(no. 32)

news of the Scots, Jan. (?),   VI, 335b*

petition of Archbishop of York, at
  Conway, to Prince Rupert, 29 Jan.,   IX(2), 432b

journey of King's sons in the West,
  16 May,   III, 195b

letters on military preparations and
  movements, June-Aug.,   XI(7), 100*

Abingdon, Ayloff's regiment transferred
  from Newport to, 15 Aug.,   VIII(1), 3a

Bedford, work on fort by levied
  laborers at, May-Sept.,   VIII(1), 3a, 5a*

Bedfordshire, orders from
  Committee of Both Kingdoms,
  21, 31 Oct.,   VIII(1), 5b*

Bolton, battle of,   IV, 266b

Breedon-on-the-Hill, engagement at,
  Apr.,   Denbigh MSS., Vol. V, 76*

Chipping Norton, King's army reported
at, 3 July,   VIII(1), 3b*

Hopton Castle, siege of,
          Bath MSS., Vol. I, 22-23, 36-40*

Lancashire, Prince Rupert to take powder
  through June,   Denbigh MSS., Vol. V, 79*

Liverpool, siege of,   I, 55b

Civil Wars, 1642-1651—History by year (covering two
    years or less)— 1644 (cont.);

Lyme, march for relief of, June,   VII(1), 2b

Marston Moor, battle of;   IV, 275b*

—; letter of Cromwell relating to
    (?), 5 July,   III, 254a

Newbury, second battle of;   VIII(1), 5b

—; newsletter relating to, etc.,   I, 51a

—; King's letter regarding(?), 3 Sept.,   II, 63a

Newport Pagnell, correspondence of
    Sir S. Luke at,   VIII(3), 12b(no. 32)

Oxford; King with forces reported
    returned to, 28 Sept.,   VIII(1), 3a*

—; see also: Parliament; at Oxford,
    1644.

Shropshire, conditions in, Apr.,
               Denbigh MSS., Vol. V, 76*

Tallabollion, militia muster of, 14 Apr.,   V, 420b

Tamworth, expected attack on,
    Mar.,   Denbigh MSS., Vol. V, 76*

Taunton, horse from Somerset ordered
    to relief of, 14 Nov.,   VI, 347a

Wem, Denbigh to advance to,
               Denbigh MSS., Vol. V, 76-77*

Civil Wars, 1642-1651—History by year (covering two
    years or less)—1644-1645; Mount Edgcumbe,
    siege and surrender of,   II, 23b

Pontefract Castle, surrender of,   VI, 461b, 462a

Civil Wars, 1642-1651—History by year (covering two
    years or less)—1646 (cont.);
    Lichfield, siege and surrender of,   IV, 340b, 341a
    Lynn, damages to almshouse during
        siege of,   XI(7), 102
    Newark, surrender of,   I, 45a
    Oxford; "blocking up" of, Apr.,   VIII(1), 10b*
    —; surrender of, June,   II, 87b

Civil Wars, 1642-1651—History by year (covering
    two years or less)—1647; newsletters; of
    Wharton and Wm. Purefoy, Mar.-Apr.,
                                          IV, 274a, b*
    —; of Sir Arthur Hopton, Nov.,   VI, 329b-330a*
    Brampton Bryan Church and town,
        accounts for losses and rebuilding,
                                    Bath MSS., Vol. I, 41*
    Chirk Castle, burdens on,   II, 73b

Civil Wars, 1642-1651—History by year (covering two
    years or less)—1648; newsletter,
    29 Mar.,   V, 143a*
    newsletters; 18 Aug., 8 Sept.,   III, 41a*
    —; of S. Kem, Rotterdam, on movements
        of English ships, etc.,   IV, 274b-275a*
    Prince Rupert to sail to Ireland,
        26 Dec.,   IX(2), 440a
    Appleby Castle, siege of, July,   III, 86b
    Beaumaris Castle, surrender of,
        12 May,   VI, 472b
    Pembroke Castle, fighting at, 28 Mar., VII, 678a

Civil Wars, 1642-1651—History by year (covering
    two years or less)—1648 (cont.);
    Yorkshire, conditions in, July, Aug., III, 86b-87a*
    Wales, disbanding of forces in, Jan.-
    Feb.,   V, 421b

Civil Wars, 1642-1651—History by year (covering
    two years or less)—1648-1649; newsletters to
    J. Gell, 5 Sept.-22 Jan.,   IX(2), 393b-394a*
    Wressell Castle, support of garrison
    in and destruction of, Nov.-May,   III, 86b, 87a*

Civil Wars, 1642-1651—History by year (covering two
    years or less)—1649; newsletter, 6 Jan.,
                         III, 192a
    Cromwell to Major Butler on military
    arrangements, 31 May,   VIII(3), 6a (no. 34)

Civil Wars, 1642-1651—History by year (covering two
    years or less)—1650; Dunbar, battle of
    letter of Cromwell regarding (?), 4 Sept.,
                         III, 195b
    Ely, Isle of (and Lynn Regis), Sir J.
    Gell accused of conspiring to deliver up,
    Mar.,   IX(2) 396a
    Man, Isle of, Derby's reply to summons
    to surrender, 12 July,   V, 333a, 339a
    Scotland, newsletter about, 3 July,   III, 192a

Civil Wars, 1642-1651— History by year (covering two
    years or less)—1651; events,   V, 299a-b;
                      VI, 434b-436a*

Clergy (or ministers) (cont.);

    payment to minister (R. Asby) of Stratford,

      Suffolk out of first fruits and tenths,

      1652,   V, 307b*

    muster of, 1608,   II, 73b

    armor rated on, 1612,   II, 86a

    list of, at general synod of Bangor,

      1636,   V, 419b

    sequestration of, and orders concerning

      tithes, profits and salary of, 1644, VIII(1), 4a-b*

    petitions of imprisoned minister

    (R. Gifford) and wife to Committee for

    Safety of Bedford 1644(?), 1645,

                        VIII(1), 2b, 8a, 8b*

    instructions of Bishop of Lincoln to,

      for celebration of Holy Communion,

      1640,   IX(2), 432b

    queries touching oath, by clergy of

      London, temp. Car. 1,   VII, 433b

    Statutes of College of Vicars, Exeter,

      1591-1730,   VIII(3), 31b

    See also: Benefices; Bishops; Chaplains

    Lent preachers; Plundered

      ministers; Preachers; Preaching;

    Scandalous ministers.

Clergyman punished for "Jewish opinions,"

    1618,   Bath MSS., Vol. II, 67-68*

Clerk of the Hanaper; see: Hanaper, Clerk of the.

Clocks, order by Trustees for delivery of all
    remaining at Whitehall, 1649,   VII, 595a
Cloth, alnagers of; 1608,   III, 56a*
    1611 (12)   III, 59a
Cloth trade; 1617,   I, 57a
    decay of, 1622,   XII(4), 464
    rates, etc., on cloth,   VI, 222b, 310b, 311a
    breaches of regulations in, 1645,   III, 86a
    cloth workers,   VI, 472a*; VII, 576b, 677a
    export; reversion of, to Buckingham,
    1621,   II, 59b
    —; to France; 1604,   III, 52b
    —; —; Mar., 1604 (05),   III, 52b-53a*; VI, 311a
    rivalry with Spanish Netherlands in,
    1611-1612,   X(1), 534-598, passim*
    See also: Wool.

Clothiers,   III, 191b; V, 403b; VII, 576b

Clothing and dress; expenses for;
    1606-1658, Rutland MSS., Vol. IV, 458-541, passim*
    —; by Northumberland, 1606-1616,
        VI, 229a-231a, passim*
    for Lady Valentia's funeral in Dublin,
    1641,   VI, 424b-425a*
    men's;   Bath MSS., Vol. II, 127*
    —; to be worn on meeting King, 1603, VII, 542b*
    —; inventory of, 1614,   III, 63a
    —; details of,   V, 394b, 397a; VII, 528a*, 530b;
        Egmont MSS., Vol. I, 102, 261*, 302

Clothing and dress; men's (cont.);

—; tailors' and other bills for,

IV, 343a, b*; VIII(2), 55a*;

IX(2), 389a; Egmont MSS., Vol. I, 345-347*, 475

—; list of "blacks," 1614, II, 8b

—; mourning apparel, V, 391a, b; V, 395a*

—; livery, VI, 326b; VII, 458b-459a*; IX(2), 423a

—; of "auncient bearer" (ensign bearer), V, 412b

—; velvet and taffeta at given prices for

Garter robes, 1607, V, 408

women's;

III, 44a; IV, 261b*; V, 389a, 389b-390a*, 394a, 397b;

XII(4), 498*; Bath MSS., Vol. II, 84*;

Egmont MSS., Vol. I, 530*

—; inventory of, 1622, VIII(2), 29b

—; costume for boy player, 1617, II, 47a*

children's, V, 392a, 393b, 395b, 397b

See also: Jewelry; Wardrobe, Royal.

Coaches; excessive use of, temp. Car. 1, I, 34a

for attendance on Spanish ambassador, III, 288b

bills for repairs to King's "caroches,"

chariots, 1624, 1625, VI, 326b

styles in, and livery of pages, 1652,

VII, 458b-459a*

Coal trade; petitions, etc., of Mayor and

people of Newcastle regarding, 1605, VI, 222b

complaints, etc., regarding coal and, 1638,

VI, 223a

abuses by Guild of Hoastmen, VI, 311b

Coal trade (cont.);

  appeal of Corporation of Hoastmen regarding

    farm of customs in, 1642,   VIII(2), 59a-b

    fine for lease of duties in, 1620,   II, 58a (no. 322)

Coals; service of carting, 1607,   VII, 668b

  ordered from Chester by Council in

    Ireland, Feb., 1641 (42),   V, 350a

Cochineal worth weight in silver, 1659,   VII, 461b

Cock-fighting at Greenwich, 1605,   VII, 668a

Cofferer of Prince's house, money paid to,

    1611, 1612,   VII, 670a

Coin; temp. Jac. 1(?),   IX(2), 366b

  coining, through 17th cent.,

        VIII(1), 74b-75a; VIII(3), 12a

  speech of Sir T. Roe on, 1640,   VIII(1), 91a

  scarcity of, 1620 (?),   III, 64b*

  alteration of the; to 1615,   IX(2), 366a

  —; 1626, including speech of Sir R.

    Cotton, 2 Sept.,

      III, 186b, 211b; IV, 408b, 410a; VIII(3), 20a

  moneys coined in Tower,

    (1603)-Feb.,

    1613,   IX(2), 366a

  indenture for making of gold pieces,

    1604,   VI, 311b

  value of silver money, 1612,   VI, 312a

  brass money to be coined, 1640,   III, 82a; VI, 352a

Coin (cont.);

See also: Gold; Mint, the; Plate.

Colonies; commission of Charles I for
    making laws for, 1634,   III, 213a
    reports, treaties, discoveries, etc., relating
    to South Seas, West Indies, South America,
    to 1768,   V, 244a
    Association (Tortuga), tobacco sent from,
    1634,   VII, 549a
    Bahamas, attack by Spanish on,
    1640,   Finch MSS., Vol. I, 51-58*
    Barbados; letter from R. Gregory in, 1641,
                       VII, 435b
    —; letters of T. Pengelly, (1650's),   VII, 691b
    Bermuda and Bermuda Company, temp. Jac. 1 -
    Car. 1,   VIII (2), 31a-49b, passim*; V, 340b
    Florida, proposed colonization of, 1641,
                     VIII(2), 49b
    Fonseta (Fonseca) Island, proposed expedition
    to,   VIII(2), 48b-49a
    Henrietta (St. Andrew's) Island,   VIII(2), 49b*
    Jamaica, 1656-1657,   VII, 575a-b
    Madagascar, proposal to colonize, Mar.,
    1637(38),   VI, 283b
    New England; orders at meetings of Council for,
    1622-1623,   IV, 370a
    —; list of ministers settled in, 1630-
    1670,   III, 366a
    —; Sir R. Saltonstall at Watertown

Colonies ; New England (cont.);

Colonies; Virginia (cont.);

for items connected with, 1606-
1613, VI, 229a-230a*

—; official papers relating to;
1607(?)- IV, 237a

—; —; 1609-1621, relating to voyages,
financial accounts, tobacco, etc., V, 340b-341b

—; exploration of Capt. Newport in,
1607, III, 54a*

—; report from Council at Jamestown,
22 June, 1607, III, 53b-54a*

—; 6th article of instructions to Lieutenant-
Governor of, 1609, V, 226b

—; patent of James I for, 1609, I, 54b

—; relation of George Percy, 1609-1612,
VI, 307b-308a

—; governor's ration in, 1611, III, 58a-b

—; Spanish activities against,
X(1), 576, 583, 600, 608-609*

—; papers of Virginia Company of London,
etc., relating to, 1612-1624,
VIII(2), 31a-48a, passim*

—; lottery for, in Surrey, (Council letter)
1614, VII, 670b

—; shipment of tobacco and use as
currency, 1620, 1634, V, 341a, b

plan for royal profits from customs of, 1620,
II, 57a (2 Feb.)

—; George Thorpe in, 1620-1634, V, 341a-b

Common Pleas, Court of, see: Court of Common
    Pleas.

Commonwealth and Protectorate, public affairs in
    period of, 1649-1660 (cont.);
    events, Mar., 1659-Mar.,
      1660,   Bath MSS., Vol. II, 128-144*
    declaration by George Booth against the
      Parliamentary government, 1659 (60),   II, 81a
    activities of Monck,   V, 361a-b; VI, 451b, 466a-b
    oath to Charles II, Feb., 1660,   IX (2), 494a*
    letter from Charles at Brussels and from
      Duke of York at Breda, Apr., 1660,
                          VIII (3), 6b, 7a
    return of Charles II, May, 1660,   V, 259b
    letters to and from Winchelsea, May,
      1660,   Finch MSS., Vol. I, 78-80*
    the Lords' letter of welcome to Charles II,
      May, 1660,   III, 90a*
    See also: Foreign relations; Parliamentary
    affairs; Parliamentary proceedings.

Communion; preparation for,   V, 418a
    instructions for celebrating, 1640,   IX (2), 432b
    to be taken by royal servants and all
      who travel or come from abroad, (1605),
                         VII, 526b*
Communion table, placing of,   III, 214a*
Companies; see: names of particular guilds, e.g.,
    Brewers; Clothiers.
Composition (or compounding); Privy Council order
    concerning, 18 May, 1605,   IV, 331a
    for wardship, 1603,   VII, 667b

Composition (or compounding) (cont.);

for aid for knighting of Prince Henry,
1608,   V, 408a

for not attending coronation, 1630,   V, 345b

for tithes in King's Forest of Exmoor,
1633,   VI, 472a

See also: Delinquents; Household, Royal;
Knighthood; Recusants.

Composition for Alienations, Office of, temp.
Jac. 1,   III, 214a

Conduct of life; instructions by Northumberland
to his son, 1609(?),   VI, 301b

precepts by W. Heveningham, temp.
Car. 1 (?),   IX(2), 369b

Congregations; see: Conventicles.

Constable; accounts of, Wirksworth,
1655,   IX(2), 395b

rotation of office of, at Worksop,   VI, 450a*

duties of, at assizes, temp. Jac. 1 or
Car. 1,   VIII(1), 27b; IX(2), 370b (no. 52, 54)

to give notice of musters,   VII, 675b

orders for "waring of carts" for King's use,
temp. Jac. 1 or Car. 1,   IX(2), 370b (no. 51)

to search for firearms, etc., (1604),   IX(2), 370a

impress men for army, (1643),   VII, 577b

to collect for relief of maimed soldiers
and seamen and for prisoners in jails,
1651,   V, 403b

Conventicles, remonstrance of city of
London against, 26 May, 1646,   V, 213b (no. 83)

Cookery; recipes for,   III, 121b;
V, 366a; VI, 420a; VIII (3), 19b (no. 61)

quinces for marmalade,   V, 369b

cake "to choose King and Queen with,"
(Twelfth Night),   V, 390a

venison for "porrage," 1657,   IX (2), 495a*

Corn; export of, forbidden, 1629,   I, 57b

Council letters regarding, 1630,
1631,   I, 57b; VI, 472a

scarcity of,   V, 314a

raising of,   V, 388b, 421b

in Virginia, (i.e. maize),   V, 341a

Cornwall, Duchy of, revenue of,
1633-1634,   VIII (3), 12a

Corporation property delivered to Mayor of
Stafford, list of, including charters,
silver, records, etc., 1622,   IV, 327a

Council, Privy; see: Privy Council.

Council of Peers at York, 1640; see: York,
Council of Peers at, 1640.

Council of Richard Cromwell, Journal of,
3 Sept., 1658-22Mar., 1658 (59),   III, 198a

Council of State, summons from its Committee
for the Affairs of Ireland and Scotland to a
conference "about the boats," Nov., 1650,
         IX (2), 441b

Court of High Commission (cont.);

    by, ca. 1623,   III, 286b and XII (4), 469-470*

    judgment against, petitioned for by objector to

    "innovations,"   VI, 352b

Court of King's Bench, controversy with Council

    of the Marches of Wales, 1606 (?),   III, 53b

Court of Probate of Wills, civilians as

    judges in,   VII, 432b

Court of Wards, arrears from, to be brought to

    Committee of Revenue, 1649,   IX (2), 434b

Courts—Ecclesiastical; proposed changes in

    jurisdiction of, Feb., 1609 (10),   III, 57b

    charge proposed for King's seal for cases in,

    Mar., 1609 (10), 1611,   III, 57b, 58a

    petitioning by Puritans against, 1603,   III, 52a

    prohibitions affecting, 1611,   IX (2), 366a

Courts—Manorial; of Sir F. Barrington at

    Clavering, 1626,   VII, 543b*

Courts of justice; Ellesmere on statutes and

    authority of, temp. Jac. 1,   III, 211b

    grounds of prohibition to, temp. Jac. 1,

        VIII (3), 20b

    Sergeant Fleetwood's "relation and opinion

    of,"   VI, 351a

    See also: Admiralty, Court of; Assizes;

    Courts—Ecclesiastical; Eyre, Lord Chief

    Justice in; Judges; Juries; Justice, adminis-

    tration of; Justices of the peace; Law and

    legal affairs; Star Chamber.

Convenant, Solemn League and, 1643;

    Denbigh's troops to take, Nov., 1643,

                                        IV, 263a-b*

    taken by (a city) in Cornwall (?), 4 Oct.,

        1643,   VII, 565b

    taken by the Lords on 15 Oct., 1643,   V, 313b

    statement of doctrines of, 1644(?),   III, 86a

    petition of inhabitants of Norfolk for

      peace according to, Sept., 1644,   XI(7), 101*

    are those who compound bound to take ?,

      1645,   VII, 453a

    only Scots adhere to, 1647,   VI, 329b-330a*

Covenanters; see: Bishops' War, First; Bishops'
    War, Second.

Creditors; see: Debts and debtors.

Crime; see: Murderers; Punishments;
    Robbers.

Crosses, trial in Star Chamber for pulling down of,
    (1614),   III, 63a

Crown lands; temp. Jac. 1,

        V, 345b, 416b; VI, 311b; VII, 593a, 668a, 669a

    temp. Car. 1;   V, 421b; VII, 577a*

    —; official papers of Lord Keeper Coventry,

                                   I, 34a

    grants of, to Scots,   V, 323b

    surveys and sales of, 1649-1655,   V, 403b, 407a;

      VII, 688a-b*; IX(2), 395b; Finch MSS., Vol. I, 73-74

    arrears to be paid to Cromwell, 1657,   III, 88a*

    "general index to," 1650-   ,   V, 259a

Crown lands (cont.);

Death rate (cont.);

from plague; Chester, June, 1647-Apr.,

    1648,   V, 339b

—; Shrewsbury,

    1650,   V, 342b-343a

Debts and debtors; warrant for protection

    against creditors,   I, 34b

records of Tally Courts, temp. Jac. 1,   VIII(3), 22a

interest on debts, and "bands" on debtors,

    1606,   Finch MSS., Vol. I, 37

King's commission for relief of prisoners for

    debt in London and Surrey, 1624,   VIII(1), 2b

See also: Usury.

Debts of the Crown, 1605, 1624, IX(2), 423a-b*, 426b

Debts to the Crown; commission for levying, May,

    1628,   XII(4), 485*

grievances, temp. Jac. 1,   IX(2), 365a

Defenses; catalogue of, 1617,   II, 8a

letters about, 1625,   III, 39b, 40a

plans of Parliament for, Jan.-Mar.,

    1641 (42),   III, 84b*

records collected by Sir R. Cotton

    regarding,   III, 215a

See also: Army and militia; Bishops'

War(s); Civil Wars; Establishment,

the; Garrisons; Naval and maritime affairs.

Delinquents; legal measures against,

        III, 266a; IX(2), 393a

settlement of debts, losses, legacies involving,

Delinquents (cont.);

                      II, 67b; III, 87b; VIII (2), 63a

list of, Mar., 1655,   VII, 460b

composition of,   III, 192a, 265b; VII, 687b*

Commissioners for Compounding with,

  (proclamation), 1647,   V, 390b

fines, etc.; 1648,   II, 9b

—; 1649,   III, 258a

—; 1646,   XII (5), 2

Sir Henry Bagot and family, 1634-1656, IV, 338b

J. Baines,   VII, 687a

Duke of Buckingham,   IV, 256b*

H. Creswick, license to, 1646,   V, 323a

Piers Edgcumbe, 1646,   II, 23a

Sir R. Graham, restoration of real estate to,

  1648,   VI, 323a

Sir H. L'Estrange,   XI (7), 104

Sir R. Leveson,   V, 142b-143a, 145b*

J. Pershouse and others, composition and

  question of sequestration of, 1649-1651,V, 298a, b

John Preston of "Turnies," Lancs., 1653,

                          VII, 687a

R. Tatton, 1649,   V, 352b-353a

See also: Royalists abroad; Sequestrations.

Denization, warrants, etc., for letters of,

  temp. Car. 1,   I, 34a

Depopulations by conversion of arable land

  into pasture,   I, 34a

Diamonds, bills of sale of, 1616, 1619, VIII (2), 29a*

Diaries, journals and memoirs; negotiations
of Treaty with Spain, 1604, VIII(1), 95a-98a*
matters connected with Jewel-House,
1641-1652, VII, 595b
siege of Manchester, Sept., 1642, V, 142a-b*
siege of Bristol, 1643, IX(2), 435a
sieges of Latham House, 1643, 1644, I, 48b
sieges of Brampton Bryan Castle, 1643,
1644, Bath MSS., Vol. I, 1-7, 22-33*
siege of Hopton Castle, 1644,
Bath MSS., Vol. I, 22-33*
Lady Anne Clifford, countess of Dorset, after-
wards countess of Pembroke, 1603-1619
and 1652-1658, III, 198a
Capt. John Hodgson's narrative of the Civil
Wars and his own afflictions, 1642-1665,
III, 121b
Sir William Monson, from fleet in the
Narrow Seas, 8-24 June, 1635, III, 191a
George Manners, 7th Earl of Rutland, during
First Bishops' War, 1639, XII(4), 504-516*
Northumberland's voyages, 1636, 1637,
III, 73b-74a; VI, 304a, 314b
Sir Fulwar Skipwith, Bart. (b. 1628) of
Newbold Hall, V, 366a
Sir Ralph Verney, Dec., 1646-Apr.,
1648, VII, 450a
Robert Woodford, steward of Northampton,
in Northampton and London, 1637-1641,
IX(2), 496-499*

Diaries, journals and memoirs (cont.);

Duels (cont.);

    Baynton-Rich duel, 1640(?),   VIII(2), 56b*

    See also: Trial by combat.

Dunkirkers; action against,   I, 43b; VII, 530b*;

                            VIII(1), 215b, 216a*

    reported off the coast, 1625,   III, 39b, 40a

Dutch war; see: War with the Dutch, 1651.

    1654,

Duties; see: Customs duties.

Dyeing of silk, abuses in rates of, 1620,

                          XII(4), 457-460*

Dyes (cochineal worth weight in silver),

    1659,   VII, 461b

East India Company (Dutch), award by

    arbitrators between England and, 1654, IV, 236a

East India Company (English);   III, 64b-65a

    petition for damages from,   III, 286b

    case of Skinner vs.,   III, 184a

    debt to money-lender, 1618,   IX(2), 425b

    dividends owing to Earl of Bristol,

    1640(?),   VIII(1), 217b

    See also: Trade, foreign—With particular

    countries, East Indies.

Easter dues, 1609, 1614,   II, 72b

Eastern Association; official papers of,

                VIII(2), 59b-62b, passim*

    expected attack on, 22-23 June, 1644, IV, 267b*

    dissensions in, July, 1644,   IV, 270a*

Eastern Association (cont.);
   army of Fairfax not to be quartered in,
     Mar., 1646(47),   IV, 274a
Ecclesiastical affairs;   VIII(3), 23b
   Divinity Lecture at Ashbourne, co. Derby,
     founded 1631 and 1632,   IX(2), 394b
   first fruits and tenths and yearly value
   of ecclesiastical properties, temp. Car.
     1,   VIII(3), 17b
   commutation of penance by distribution to
     poor, 1630,   V, 418b
   forty non-conformists imprisoned, (1632),
                        VII, 548a
   Committee for Ejecting Scandalous Ministers
     and Schoolmasters,   IX(2), 395b-396a*
   in Bermuda, 1612-1634,
        VIII(2), 31b-34b, passim, 36b-38a, passim*
   propositions of Commissioners from Ireland
     at Oxford, 1644,   Egmont MSS., Vol. I, 212-229*
   petition of J. Williams, Bishop of Lincoln,
     2 Oct., 1640,   IX(2), 432b
   in Diocese of Norwich,   VII, 432a; VIII(3), 30b
   See also: Benefices; Churches; Clergy;
     Conventicles; Court of High Commission;
     Courts—Ecclesiastical; Pluralities;
     Protestantism; Scotland, relations with;
     Sects; Tithes.

Ecclesiastical Causes, Court of High Commission
   for, 1559-1641; see: Court of High Commission.

Ecclesiastical Causes, Commissioners for; form
of oath to be taken by, 1611, III, 58a
appointment of, for Diocese of Exeter,
1626, III, 68a-b*

Ecclesiastical courts; see: Courts—Ecclesiastical.

Education; expenses; for books, etc., for Con O'
Neal, (O'Neill), 1617, III, 265a
—; of Northumberland for teaching and for
sons at school and university,
1603-1616, VI, 228b-231a*
—; for schooling and diet of boys, 1646,
Egmont MSS., Vol. I, 300*
—; of J. Perceval, student at Cambridge,
1647, Egmont MSS., Vol. I, 474-475*
—; of R. Eaton, tutor at Brasenose,
1658-1663, VI, 420b*
T. Finch, student of civil law at Padua,
writes home, 1605, Finch MSS., Vol. I, 35*
W. Rokeby on disciplining children,
1609(?), VI, 449b
T. Hobbes' recommendations for the son of the
Earl of Devonshire, 1648, IX(2), 439b*
young son of Edmund Perceval to be sent to
Ireland to train as clerk, 1639,
Egmont MSS., Vol. I, 112*

See also: Schools; Universities.

Elections—Municipal; 1614, III, 62b, 63a
in London, Oct. (?), 1640, XII(4), 524*

Entertainment of royalty (cont.);

expenses for King and Prince Charles on
progresses, etc., 1615-1622,   III, 264b

visit of James I to Stafford, 1617,   IV, 327a

visit of Marie de' Medici to London,
1638,   IX(2), 497b

See also: Progresses, royal.

Entertainments; see: Amusements.

Epigrams; see: Biographical notes.

Escheators, warrants for appointment of,   I, 34a

Establishment, the (i.e. list of nobility,
royal officials, defenses, etc.);

             I, 31a, 49a; II, 8a, III, 63a

See also: Nobility; Officials—Royal and State.

Estates; forfeited. See: Sequestrations.

Estates; landed. See: Landed estates.

Evil, King's; see: King's evil.

Exchange, proposition for the King's,
temp. Jac. 1,   IX(2), 366b

Exchequer, papers on the, 1650,   VIII(3), 10a

Exchequer, Barons of the, speech of Sir Edward
Hyde relating to, 1640,   IX(2), 432b

Expeditions; see: Cadiz expedition, 1625; Gibraltar,
proposed expedition to, 1632; La Rochelle,
siege and expeditions; Man, Isle of, expedition
against; Voyages and travel; West Indies
expedition, Prince Rupert's, 1651-1653;
West Indies expedition, 1654-1655.

Eyre; office of Lord Chief Justice in,   XII(4), 495

Eyre (cont.);

　　See also: Forests.

Fairs and markets; Llangollen recommended for a
　　fair,　　　　　　　　　　　　II, 67a (14 Jac. 1)
　　at Hatfield, 1613, 1644,　　　VII, 543b; VII, 569b*
　　space provided for an open market in
　　　　London,　　　　　　　　　　　III, 192b
　　St. Georges' fair, Northampton, 1638, IX (2), 497a
　　stallage fees in Pontefract, 1614,　　VI, 462a-b

Farming; see: Agriculture.
Farming of the customs; see: Customs duties.
Fast, a general; 1628,　　　　　　　XII (4), 484*
　　1646,　　　　　　　　　　　　V, 390b (no. 57)

Fees; for baronage, 1603,　　　　　　II, 19b
　　for knighthood, to be paid to King's
　　　servants, 1626,　　　　　　　　V, 140b
　　payable on commission for cavalry and
　　　infantry,　　　　　　　　　　IV, 262b
　　Bishop of Exeter accused of extortion of,
　　　1628,　　　　　　　　　　　　IX (2), 428b
　　taken by judges,　　　　　　　　III, 192b
　　to the master of the King's jewels,
　　　1644,　　　　　　　　　　　　IX (2), 435b
　　of the Fleet (prison),　　　　　　III, 213b
　　of physicians;
　　　　　　Rutland MSS., Vol. IV, 454-522, passim*
　　—; surgeons and apothecaries, 1618, IX (2), 425b*
　　inquiry into exacted fees and innovated

Fees (cont.);

    offices; 1623,   III, 213b

    —; temp. Car. 1,   III, 69a*, 70b, 71b

    of palace housekeepers and wardrobers,

        1625,   II, 81a

    of the Household and Revenue officers,

        1628,   III, 265a-b

    of solicitor-general, 1648,   III, 288b

    of "sergeant ancient," 1634,   III, 265b

    See also: Officials —Royal and State; Wages.

Fen drainage;   VI, 311a; XI (7), 100;

                  Lothian MSS., p. 84, 85*

    lands from, claimed by Queen, 1635, VIII (1), 209b

Finance, public; report to House of Commons

        on, (1658) -1659,   XV (1), 96 -105*

    Council advice to King on reducing expenses,

      Dec., 1617,   III, 196b and Bath MSS., Vol. II, 66*

    report on the demand upon the Commission for the

      Sale of the King's Goods, Dec.,

      1651,   III, 291a

    King's debts, pensions, fees, 1616,   V, 355a

    revenue and debts of England, Scotland and

      Ireland, 1654,   VII, 687a

    warrant of R. Cromwell for Ł6000 for "the

      public contingencies," 30 Dec., 1658, VIII (3), 6b

    See also: Accounts (receipts and expenses) —

    Public; Benevolences and loans to the

    King; Civil Wars, 1642-1651 —Finance —

    Parliamentary; Civil Wars, 1642-1651 —

Finance, public; See also (cont.);
    Finance—Royalist; Loan from London companies;
    Revenue; Taxation.

Fines; due from Earl of Northumberland,
                                        III, 59b*, 59b-60a
    articles and petitions concerning
    ecclesiastical,   III, 56b*, 58a
Fish; provisions of, 1634,   XII (4), 495*
    from Newfoundland (charter party),
    1604,   VI, 310b

Fisheries; report on, Sept., 1631,   III, 71a*
    Dutch, in English waters; encroachment of,
    (1635),   III, 71b*
    —; licenses demanded of,
    1636-1637,   III, 72a-75a, passim*
    —; claim of, Dec., 1618,   III, 190b
    French, on English coast,
    Feb., 1620,   II, 57b (no. 299)
Fishing; proclamation of King regarding,
    6 May, 1609,   IX (2), 365b
    grant of rights of,   V, 417b, 418b
    right of Queen to grant licenses for,
    1614,   IX (2), 365b
    licenses registered at Brussels for,
    temp. Car. 1,   IX (2), 440b
    abuses of, in Thames, 1630,   VII, 592b
    patent for, 1633,   V, 355b
    certification of, relating to fishing
    craft, 7 Mar., 1634,   V, 413a

Five members, action against the, 1641,

I, 51a; V, 333b, 344a

Flag for Navy, 1649, V, 307b*

Flesh, eating of, at forbidden times, I, 34a;

V, 352a, 401b, 402a; VI, 223b; VII, 669b*;

VIII (2), 51a; Lothian MSS., p. 83

Flour mills, lease of, at Kilmainham, to Sir
John Temple, 1642, Egmont MSS., Vol. I, 186-188*

Fodder; seaweed to be used for, III, 191a

supplies and prices of hay and oats,

V, 403a, 410a; VI, 231b

Food and drink; expenses for,

Rutland MSS., Vol. IV, 447-541, passim*

expenses of Northumberland for,

1603-1616, VI, 228b-231a, passim

accounts; for wines, etc. (household of
Shrewsbury?), 1603, VI, 450a

—; for food for a large establishment,

1617-1629, VIII (1), 277b

prices of; IV, 336b

—; game, cattle, sheep, poultry, and farm
produce, 1601-1608, IV, 414a*

—; flesh and bread, 1622, V, 410a

—; flour, 1647, Egmont MSS., Vol. I, 362*

—; sweet meat, 1657-1658, IX (2), 370b

provisions of fish and fowl, XII (4), 495*

diet books of Lords of Council,

1602, 1605, 1635, IX (2), 413a

diet for Queen and servants at Hampton

Food and drink (cont.);

Foreign relations—France treaty (cont.);

Netherlands, 1603, III, 52a

—; secret article for expulsion of
Charles II and others from France,
and certain Frenchmen from England,
1654, VIII(3), 6a

—; agreement of Cromwell with
Mazarin, 1657(?), VIII(1), 29b

—; private articles between the King
of France and the Protector, 10 May, 1657,

V, 314a

ambassadors and envoys; allowances for
French ambassador, VII, 592b

—; Sir T. Edmondes; his state papers
and correspondence, temp. Jac. 1, VIII(3), 10a

—; —; his replacement by Beecher,
1607, VII, 592a

—; —; his letters to Sir J. Digby,
1611-1612, X(1), 521-614, passim*

—; —; his tour in France, 1614, III, 292b

—; list of train of Duc de Bouillon,
1612, XII(4), 436-437*

—; Montague sent for news of Louis
XIV, III, 287b

—; letter of J. Selden to E. Herbert,
1619, V, 312b

—; negotiations of Bassompierre, 1626,
and of Du Moulin, 1627, III, 189b

—; letters of Sir I. Wake at Paris,

Foreign relations—Oldenburg; safeguard to Count,
12 Feb., 1651(52), III, 192a

Foreign relations—Palatinate; see: Palatinate.

Foreign relations—Papacy; ambassador (Captain
Brett) sent by Charles I, 1635, VI, 466a
treatment of W. Montagu at Rome,
1636, Denbigh MSS., Vol. V, 19*

Foreign relations—Poland; Latin oration to
James I by ambassador from Poland,
Jan., 1621, V, 410a
instructions to Sir Thomas Roe, 1629, III, 190b
letter of John Bale on Poland, 1632, VIII(3), 10a
proposal by King of Poland for
Princess Palatine, 1634, VIII(3), 5b(no. 23)
league with Sweden against Poland
proposed, Apr., 1635, III, 191a

Foreign relations— Portugal; treaty; 29 Jan.,
1642, III, 136a
—; and powers to ambassadors,
1652-1656, VI, 309a
—; 10 July, 1654, III, 132b; IV, 248b

Foreign relations—Russia; Sir R. Lee,
ambassador to, VII, 527b

Foreign relations—Savoy; letter of Prince Charles
to Duke, June, 1613, IX(2), 425a
commission and letters of Sir I. Wake,
(Dec., 1614)-Oct., 1623, III, 190a

Foreign relations—Savoy (cont.);

correspondence of Lord Feilding (afterwards
Earl of Denbigh); 1635-1643, VI, 277a-287a*
—; 29 June, 1638 - 28 Oct., 1639,
Denbigh MSS., Vol. V, 58-68*
demands of Sir T. Killigrew, Nov., 1649, IX(2), 441a
treatment of W. Montagu at (Turin),
Denbigh MSS., Vol. V, 19*
See also: Protestants in the Savoy.

Foreign relations—Spain; temp. Jac. 1, VII, 516a, b;
IX(2), 369b
correspondence of Kings of England
and Spain and others, temp. Jac. 1,
II, 46a (vol. clxxviii)
arming of a fleet by the King with
assistance of the King of Spain, (n. d.),
V, 312b
letters to the King of Spain relating to
injuries to merchants trading to
Malaga, (n. d.), V, 313a
Spanish-Dutch activities in the Downs,
III, 77b*
peace with Spain; discourse of Sir Walter
Raleigh on, III, 212a; VII, 516a; IX(2), 386a
—; speech of Sir E. Cecil against, III, 66a*
—; reasons against, 1603, VII, 591b
case of ship "Vineyard," 1605-1621,
VIII(1), 213a, b
correspondence of Privy Council and

Foreign relations—Spain (cont.);

Foreign relations—Venice; ambassadors and envoys
(cont.);

—; honors due ambassadors to Venice,
1609, 1610,   VIII(2), 102b-103a
—; letters of Sir D. Carleton to Sir J.
Digby, 1611-1612,   X(1), 521-608, passim*
—; Sir I. Wake's embassy; Jan.,
1624(25),   VIII(2), 29b
—; —; 1627,   II, 44a (vol. xcv)
—; Feilding's embassy; instructions for,
1636,   VIII(2), 54b
—; —; debts of,
            VI, 287b; Denbigh MSS., Vol. V, 75-76*
—; correspondence of Feilding and Sir G.
Talbot during their embassies, 1634-
1643,   VI, 277a-287a;
            Denbigh MSS., Vol. V, 9-76, passim*

Foreign relations—Württemberg; investing of
Duke with Order of the Garter,   II, 20a; VI, 311a
Foreign service (i.e., military service under
foreign countries); attempts of Sir T. Barrington
and J. Barrington to join,
            VII, 544a, 546b, -546a, passim*
F. Wilson, serving with Dutch and Swedes,
temp. Car. 1,   V, 305a
C. Fairfax serving under Goring in Low
Countries, 1636,   IX(2), 431a
casualties at Breda, 1637,   VII, 677b

Foreigners in England (cont.);

    church attendance of their children

      ordered, 1634,   III, 212a

    proposal to tax, 1652,   III, 192a

Forests; privileges, limits, customs of,

    temp. Jac 1,   VIII(3), 30b

fee deer in, temp. Jac. 1, Finch MSS., Vol. I, 41*

Earl of Sussex said to have had custody

    of records of, 1611,   Finch MSS., Vol. I, 39*

swain moot court, 1623,   VII, 674b

grievances regarding, co. Berks, 1640,

                          IX(2), 390b

Ashdown, abuses in, 1607,   V, 304b

Braden, placita forestae, 20 Aug.,

    (1611),   III, 211b

Dean;   VIII(3), 10a

—; proceedings in Eyre, 10 July,

    1634,   III, 185b, 211b, 213a

—; rioters in, to be proceeded

    against, 14 July, 1631,   III, 190b

Exmoor, compounding for tithes in,

    1633,   VI, 472a

New Forest, justice seat at Winchester,

    Sept., 1608,   III, 211b

The Peak, stag to be taken in, 1609,

                      XII(4), 417*

Pickering, fee stag demanded from,

    1613,   XII(4), 441-442

Garden plants (cont.);

  "tallopp" (tulip?),   IX(2), 386a

  See also: Trees.

Garrisons; at Scottish Border, 4 Feb., 1616,

                                     II, 52a

  Berwick garrison; Aug., 1640,   III, 82b

  —; allotment for, temp. Jac. 1,   VI, 311b

  —; expenses at, 1630(?),   III, 71a

  —; officers and troops at, Dec., 1639,   III, 79a

  —; —; their wages, Jan., 1639(40),   III, 80b

  Malmesbury garrison, relief of,

    1657(?),   III, 88b

  See also: Army and militia; Civil Wars,

    1642-1651—Armies.

Garter, Order of the; see: Order of the Garter.

Gentlemen harbingers,   VII, 592a

Gentlemen pensioners, subsidy for, 1625,

                           IX(2), 426b*

  Ł150 due Sir R. More for services,

    temp. Car. 1,   VII, 678b

Gentry; names of Suffolk nobility and,

    1560-1604,   IX(2), 371b

    definition of an esquire,   VI, 459b

Gibraltar, proposed naval expedition to

    Straits of, 1632,   III, 71a

Glass; importation to be forbidden,   I, 34a

    windows made in Chester at 5d. a foot,

    1653,   Egmont MSS., Vol. I, 528*

Gunpowder (cont.);

Hanaper, Clerk of the, temp. Car. 1, VI, 322a, 323a

Harbingers, Gentlemen; see: Gentlemen Harbingers.

Harbor; Sandgate suggested as a, 1656,   V, 313a
   causes of decay of Rye Haven,   V, 407a

Hawking and hawks;   XII (4), 421-422*
   hawks' meat,   XII (4), 469
Hay; price of, 1637,   VI, 231b
   loan of, to be returned two fold, 1630,   V, 396b
Heralds, cases in courts against, 1622,   III, 286b
Hidage, 1633,   II, 18b (no. 43)

High Commission for Ecclesiastical Causes,
   Court of; see: Court of High Commission.
Highways, 1621;   Rutland MSS., Vol. IV, 217*
   maintenance of, at Allington, co. Lincoln,
    1628,   XII (4), 487
   right of way for public path and highway in
    co. York, 1640,   VI, 424b

Hoastmen; see: Coal trade.
Horse racing,   IX (2), 389a; XII (4), 454, 456*
Horses; breeding of,   VI, 327b; XII (4), 491*
   their export to Count of Joinville without a
    license, temp. Jac. 1 or Car. 1, II, 63a (no. 500)
   of Buckingham and of Royal Household,
    1619-1629,   VI, 323a-327b*
   grant for life to G. Hervie "to run 12 horses"
    in Havering Park, 1614,   VII, 593b
   importation of; temp. Jac. 1,
      VI, 323a; 326b; IX (2), 425b

Horses; importation of (cont.);

—; 1654,   VII, 531a

present of, to Charles I,   VIII (1), 552b*

for King's service, temp. Car. 1,   V, 402a, 413a

Earl of Northumberland's expenses

    for, 1603-1616,   VI, 228b-231a, passim*

See also: Army and militia—Supplies and pay;

Civil Wars, 1642–1651—Armies—Parliamentary

—Supplies and pay; Ireland—Rebellion of 1641

and Civil War; Stables.

Hospitals;   V, 410b; IX (2), 389a

military hospitals in Ireland,

    1643,   Egmont MSS., Vol. I, 189*

Charterhouse (Sutton Hospital); suit against,

    1612,   III, 187a

—; petition of Master of, 1628 (?),   III, 286b

—; Bacon's opinion to King James on

    employment of,   III, 215b*

—; Committee of Parliament for Hospitals

appoints Oliver Cromwell Governor of,

    1650,   VIII (2), 64a

Christ's Hospital, decree of Court to

    confirm charitable uses of, 1617,   IV, 229a

Clun and Rising,   V, 412a

Greenwich, inscription on cornerstone of,

    1613,   V, 408b

Ruthin, Bishop of Bangor's commissioner to

    visit, (n. d.),   V, 418a

St. Catherine's Hospital, allowance to S. Slater

Hospitals (cont.);

Household, Royal; officers of (cont.);
    fee, 1634,   III, 265b
  —; sergeant-at-arms, allowance of E. Birkhead
    as,   III, 288b
  —; "undertaker" (entrepreneur), Castillian
    Mason appointed as, 1620,   IV, 342b
  purveyance of provision for;   VI, 310b
  —; temp. Jac. 1,
         V, 407b-408a*; VII, 675a; XII (4), 403
  —; temp. Car. 1,
         I, 34a; V, 401b-402a; VII, 592b, 689a
  —; measures for abolishing of, temp. Jac. 1,
                 VII, 668a, 674b
  —; composition money for; (Privy Council
    order), 1610,   IV, 331a
  —; —; in Surrey,   VII, 675a
  See also: Apothecaries; Cart-taking; Chaplains
  in Ordinary; Green Cloth, Board of the;
  Stable, Royal.

Household accounts; Belvoir (Earl of Rutland),
    1602-1658,   Rutland MSS., Vol. IV, 443-541*
  Blickling Hall, 1656,   Lothian MSS.,p. 87-88*
  Flixton Hall, 1633-1634,   III, 277b
  Gorhambury, 1637-1639,   I, 13a
  L'Estrange family, 1585-1663,   III, 271a
  Longleat, 16th to end of 17th cent.,   III, 189a
  Earl of Northumberland, 1603-1629,   VI, 228-231
  Throckmorton, 1650-1750,   X (4), 169
  See also: Food and drink.

Household books; Londesborough, 1608-
1653, III, 41b
Chelsey (Chelsea?), 1630-1631, III, 41b

Household goods; articles for a raffle,
1612, Bath MSS., Vol. II, 61-62*
sale of, at "Bodwine" and Fretwell,
1618, V, 417b
shopping list for, 1647, V, 389a*
expenses for Northumberland's,
1606-1616, VI, 228a-231a*
pewter bought by the Chamber of
Marlborough, IV, 351b(no. 108)
of E. Manestie, 1625, and T. Loate,
1627, XII(4), 474, 478, 484*
"pappellnicke" ware, 1632, and kettles,
1634, XII(4), 491, 495
tamarisk cup, VII; 527a
inventories; at Alnwick, 1605, III, 53a
—; of J. Griffith, at Greenwich, 1623, V, 410b
—; of Manners family, 1632, 1642, 1651,
I, 11b
—; of Sir G. More of Losely, 1632, VII, 677a
—; of Skipton Castle, temp. Jac. 1 and
1645, III, 41b
—; at Uffington, 1608,
Rutland MSS., Vol. IV, 210*
—; of Sir Richard Wortley, III, 226a

Houses; new houses in London, builders of,
proceeded against; 1607, III, 54a

Houses; new houses in London, builders of,
    proceeded against (cont.);

—; suggestions for stopping increase of, temp.
    Jac. 1,   IX(2),386a
—; Earl of Clare's case, temp. Jac. 1 or
    Car. 1,   III,192b
—; laws and arguments,   VIII(1),98a-b*
rent; of part of Essex House, 1613
    or 1614,   VI,230a
—; of parsonage of Wargrave, Berks,
    1614,   VIII(1),283b
—; of house at Charing Cross,
    1645,   IX(2),438b*
sales; of manor house of Leconfield,
    1608,1609,   VI,229b
—; of "fyer house" or "burgage,"
    1640,1641,   III,247a
law relating to inhabiters of cottages, temp.
    Car. 1,   VIII(1),2b

Huguenots; see: Protestants in France.
Hunting; game preserved for King's;
    1619,   XII(4),456*
—; 1633,   IX(2),390a
hound,   XII(4),456
poacher; examination of, before Archbishop
    of Canterbury, 1620,   IX(2),425b
—; forbidden to keep alehouse, 1624,   IX(2),427a
poaching;   VII,667b-668a,672b;XII(4),457

Hunting; poaching (cont.);

  —; in Rochwood Hare Park, 1619,   VII, 543b
  service of "Sieur de St. Rauy" to James
    I in connection with, 1625,   IX (2), 427a, b
  of partridges, by a lady, 1654,

                  Egmont MSS., Vol. I, 559*

Husbandry; see: Agriculture.

Ice, "conserve" for snow and, 1646,   IX (2), 438b
Impositions, case of, in Parliament, temp.

    Jac. 1,   III, 254b; IV, 374a; VII, 515b
  report of Sir E. Sandys on, 1614,   VI, 451b
  on tobacco, warrant of patent of annuity from,
    1637,   I, 34b
  See also: Customs duties.

Impressment; extortion connected with,
    1624,   II, 13a
  exemption from, for sailors of the
    "Diamond," 1635 (36),   III, 71b
  of seamen; for suppression of piracy,
    1620,   III, 64b
  —; for Navy, 1653,   IX (2), 442a
  of 300 footmen, 1640,   II, 48b
  grievances regarding, 1640,   IX (2), 390b
  Fairfax ordered by King to assemble
    "pressed" troops, 1640,   VI, 467a
  pay for impressed men, 1651,   IX (2), 441b*
  of workmen of Ambrose Gray, 1640 (?), II, 48b

Inclosures; I, 34a; III, 190b

   at Hoylandswaine, 1629, III, 226a

   in Derbyshire and Leicestershire, 1607,

                      XII(4), 405, 406

   case in Star Chamber concerning, 1614, III, 63a

   at Newstead, 1616, XII(4), 448*

   at Fulbeck, 1622, 1629, XII(4), 467, 488

   in Leicester, 1630, VI, 472a

   in Lincolnshire, 1653, V, 393-394a

   offer to arbitrate question of sheepwalks,

     1629, XI(7), 96

Informations, Committee for, examinations

   at Chester for, 1642, V, 350b

Informer; reward paid to, from debt due to

   delinquent, 1646, II, 67b

   petition of T. Parmenter, 1656,

                 Lothian MSS., p. 88*

Inner Temple; masque by W. Browne at, IX(2), 386b

   certificates of admission to, I, 34b

   proceedings of Parliament of (1617),

     petitions to Bench of (1619), accounts

     of (1622), I, 34b

   account of W. Yorke, steward, 1633, IX(2), 390a

Inns; not to serve flesh in Lent, 1626, 1631,

     1633, V, 401b, 402a

   charges at, 1643, 1645, IX(2), 392a, b

Inns of Court; antiquities of, IV, 353b

   orders of judges for readers in,

Ireland—Rebellion of 1641 and Civil War— History by
 year (covering two years or less); rebels repulsed
 at "Lisnegarvy"(Lisburn), 1641,   V, 413b-414a
 commissions to seize ships of rebels,
 1641-1642,   III, 84a-b
 letters and papers of the authorities at
 Chester, and others, 1641-1642,
                      V, 344a-346b, 349a-352b, passim*
 military operations, 1642,   III, 191b
 danger to King (letter of Inchiquin),
 (1644),   VII, 235b*
 conditions in Ireland, 1646,   IV, 273b*
 votes (in Parliament) concerning, 1647, IV, 274b*
 report of E. Butler to Prince Rupert,
 26 Mar., 1649,   IX(2), 440b*
 battle of Bayatrea, 1649,   III, 192a
 Drogheda, 1649,   VII, 457a*
 newsletter, 9 June, 1651,   VII, 571a

Iron, price of, temp. Jac. 1(?),   VI, 449b

Ironmonger, petition from, to continue trade
 which supplies army, 1644(?),
                      Denbigh MSS., Vol. V, 79*
Iron works, petition concerning, at Silkstone,
 co. York, 1632,   III, 226a

Jail delivery, commissions of, temp. Car. 1,   I, 34a

Jails and prisons; rates of quarter pay for, co.
 Worcester, 1647-1654,   I, 55a

Jails and prisons (cont.);

James I; public affairs in the reign of; (cont.);

Jewel-House (cont.);

Juries, (cont.);

1612-1613, III, 56a, 59b, 60a, 61b, 62a

correct returns demanded of, co.

Gloucester, 1609, V, 345a

Justice, administration of; judicial seals

demanded by Sir Marmaduke Lloyd, 1636,

III, 258b*

"Custodes Justiciarii Angliae," VIII(3), 20a

Northern highwaymen invited to turn

state's evidence, 1629, VII, 262a-b*

order for payment of salary to Lord

Chief Justice of Upper Bench,

1649, III, 266a

See also: Assizes; Courts of justice;

Courts—Ecclesiastical; Judges; Juries;

Trial by combat; Trials.

Justices of the Peace; papers relating to, temp.

Jac. 1, III, 190b; V, 410a; VI, 311a; VII, 593b

Commission of Peace required before

jail delivery, 1643, VI, 336a

names of, 1651, VIII(3), 21a

King's Bench, Court of; see: Court of King's

Bench.

King's evil, 1629, IV, 369b

Knighthood; temp. Car. 1(?), III, 190b

order of, to be taken by all with £40 in lands

or rent, Jan., 1625, V, 411a

gentlemen called up to pay for, (1629), VII, 545b

Knighthood (cont.);

    compounding for, in Westmorland,

        1632,   VII, 689b

    fees for, (1631),   VII, 547a*

    suit for non-appearance for, (n.d.),   III, 187a

    fines for refusing, in Norfolk, 1631,   III, 272b

Knighting of Prince Henry, 1609, III, 196b; V, 408a, b;
                  VI, 229a; Bath MSS., Vol. II, 57*

Knights, created; by James I, 1603,

                        III, 185b; IV, 341a;

            VII, 245b; VII, 526a, 527b, 528a*, 329a

    by Charles I, to 1642,   VII, 245b

Knights of the Bath; list of,

    1603,   Bath MSS., Vol. II, 51

    made at creation of Henry Prince of

        Wales 1610,   IV, 363a

    fee for creation of, 12 Jac. 1,   VI, 459b

    fees from, for Royal servants, 1626,   V, 140b

Knights of the Shire; see: Elections—Parliamentary.

Labor; see: Apprentices; Wages.

Land; ejectment from Manners estate,

    1608,   XII(4), 413

    sale of, 1608,   XII(4), 409

    price of; 1629,   VI, 231a

    —; in Gwesany, etc.,

        1622,   VI, 424a

    rent of; ca. 1640,   II, 64a

    —; for pasture, 1623,   VII, 530a

    inventory of, in Norfolk, as rated and

Land (cont.);

    rented, 1610-1611.   VIII(3), 30b

    See also: Crown lands; Inclosures;

    Escheators; Hidage.

Landed estates; list of, in Northumberland,

    1625(?),   III, 67b

    particulars of,   III, 192b

    rents of Earl of Chesterfield and others,

    1643,   IX(2), 392a

    correspondence of Abel Barker as High

    Sheriff, farmer and landholder, 1642-

    1665,   V, 387-398, passim

    Sir F. Barrington's court at Clavering,

    1626,   VII, 543b

    of Sir M. Finch,

    "before 1614,"   Finch MSS., Vol. I, 42*

    of the Manor of Fotheringhay and the

    "Colledge in the county of Northampton,"

    1604,   V, 403b

    of J. Griffith, 1627,   V, 418a

    of Sir P. Perceval at Burton, Somerset, and

    in Ireland, 1637-1659,

                 Egmont MSS., Vol. I, 84-610, passim*

    reports of Sir J. Rous to Sir R. Rich,

    1606,   Finch MSS., Vol. I, 37-38*

    agreement between Earl and Countess of

    Rutland regarding Belvoir, Haddon and

    Croxton, 1648,   IX(2), 393b*

    letters of Sir J. and Lady Maynard to J. Sharp

Landed estates (cont.);

   of Little Horton, Bradford, 1649,

   1658-1665,   VIII(1),637b

   of Shirley family (rental), 1657-1665,   V,369a-b

   letter from J. Luke to Lady Smith,

   in "Lyttle St. Bartholomew,"

   1614,   VII,543b

management of; instructions for, on Northumberland

   estates, 1609,   III,109b

—; memoranda of Sir R. Throckmorton

   on, 1612-1701,   III,257a

—; appointment of steward of Furness,

   1607,   III,247a

—; report by steward of Sir F. Barrington

   at "Calborne,"   VII,543a

accounts, etc.; 1643-1645,   XII(5),1

—; of Hereford, 1638,   I,53b

—; of Longleat,   III,199b

—; of W. Heveningham, Suffolk,   IX(2),370b

—; of Earl of Northumberland;

   1603-1629,   VI,228b-231a*

—; —; Jan., 1617(18),   III,64a

—; —; losses of, in war, 1646,   III,86b

—; of Earl of Rutland; 1611,   XII(4),430-431*

—; —; 1615,   XII(4),444*

—; of J. Townley, 1601-1608,   IV,414a

—; of Earl of Warwick, 1639(?),   VIII(2),55b

See also: Rents.

Landlords; indemnity to tenants against,

Landlords (cont.);

1643, VII, 444b

La Rochelle, siege and expeditions for

relief of; 1627-1628, II, 18b (no. 43?);

III, 69a-b*, 70a, 214b; V, 412a, b; XII(4), 483*

purchase of horses for, 1627, VI, 327a

French account of landing at Rhe,

July, 1627, VII, 433a

newsletter, 11 July, 1628, VII, 543b*

letter of Henri de Rohan to King of Great

Britain about loss of "Rochell" etc.,

12 Mar., 1629, V, 312b

letter of Louis XIII describing, 4 Oct.,

1628, IX(2), 424a*

"Bref du Pape Urban VIII sur la prise

de La Rochelle," 23 Nov., 1628, V, 312b

condition of La Rochelle when King of

France entered, 1628, VI, 351b

Law and legal affairs; temp. Jac. 1 and Car. 1,

letter of Sir A. Cooper to R. I, 31a

Bankes, relating to, 1658, VIII(1), 212a

dictionary and commonplace-book, VI, 420b

note-books, commonplace-books, reports

of cases, etc., of Sir John, Sir Heneage

and W. Finch, VII, 514b-515b, passim, 517b

controversies regarding prohibitions, 1610,

IX(2), 366a-b

collections of papers concerning, VIII(3), 22b

day book of attorney, 1608-1614, III, 226a

Letter Office; see: Post Office.

Letters (collections) of general content—1603-1660,
or period not specified (cont.);

letters,	V, 312a-b
Somerset, Duchess of, and family,	III, 200a
Spencer family,	II, 18b
Thynne family,	III, 199b
Vaughan family,	IV, 360a
Verney family, 1639-1660, including news,	VII, 434b-463a*
Wilbraham family,	III, 293a-b
Wilson family and others,	V, 305a

Letters (collections) of general content—1603-
1649; miscellaneous,   VI, 305b-306a;
           VIII (3), 9b (no. 1), 13b (no. 46, 49, 50)

1606-1644, public affairs,	III, 298b
1633-1637, Roman Catholics,	III, 277a-b
Bacon, Sir F.,	II, 2b (no. 190); III, 184a, 214a

Bagot family,
       IV, 330a, 334a, 336b, 338b, 341b, 342a, 342b

Sir J. Bankes, including news,

1636-1642,	VIII (1), 211a-212a
Coningsby family, including news,	VII, 682a-b
Lord Denbigh and family,	IV, 255b-260b*
Eliot, Sir J.,	I, 43b
Hamilton, Marquis of, 1636-1641,	IV, 256b-258b*
Hertford, Earl of, 1604-1606,	III, 109b
E. Hyde to B. Whitelocke, 1636-1642,	III, 191b
James I,	IV, 374a
Northumberland and others, 1605-1614	III, 109b

Letters (collections) of general content—1603-1649
(cont.);
Northumberland, from the fleet, 1636-1637,

VI, 304a

Shrewsbury, Earls of (Talbot family),
III, 185a, 198a, 298a-299a, passim; VI, 449a-b
Whitmore and Savage, 1624-1646,   IV, 360a
R. Winwood(?) and others,   IV, 372b

Letters (collections) of general content—1642-
1660; 1645-1660,   III, 185b
1646-1652,   III, 290b-291a
1654-1660,   III, 192b
Sir Abel Barker, Bart., and family,   V, 387-398*
1646-1647, J. Rushworth to Fairfax,   IX(2), 438b
1653, J. Thurloe to Whitelocke in
London,   V, 314a

Letters (collections) on a particular topic; see:
entry under the topic, e.g., Corn, Council
letters regarding.
Letters (single letters); see: entry under subject
of the letter, e.g., Food and drink, transportation
of victuals forbidden (Council letter).
Letters of news—Of English or of general affairs—
Collections; 1603-1616, Philip Gawdy,

VII, 526a-530a*

1605-1622, T. Screven and R. Dallington,

XII(4), 395-468*

1617-1648, to Sir W. Wrottesley and
others,   II, 47a-48a*

Letters of news—Of English or of general affairs—
    Collections (cont.);
    1625-1648, from "el hombre fiel," III, 282b-283b*
    temp. Car. 1, Col. T. Davies,   III, 258a
    1625-1640, to Sir G. Manners and
      others,   XII (4), 471-524, passim*
    1626, Sir J. Whitelocke,   ·   III, 190b
    1628-1632, to Lady Johanna Barrington
      (Parliamentary, etc.),
               VII, 537b-538a; VII, 544a-548b, passim*
    1631-1660, S. Charlton to Sir R. Leveson,
                         V, 160-167*
    1632-1660, Sir T. Gower,   V, 191a-194b*
    1632-1647, from Charles Louis, Count
    Palatine, and others,   III, 116b-117a
    1635-1642 (43), to Feilding in Italy,   VI, 277-287*
    1638-(39)-1645(?), from F. Godolphin,   II, 99a
    1639-1660, F. Newport to Sir R. Leveson,
                        V, 147, 151*
    1639-1640, Northumberland to Leicester,
            III, 77a-79b, 80a-83a, passim*
    1640-1660, Verney family,   VII, 434b-463a*
    1640-1642, Cumberland (Clifford) family,
                           II, 19b
    1640-1641, Egmont MSS., Vol. I, 119-122, 132-133*
    1642-1660, the Langleys,   V, 178-182*
    1642-1660, Newport family,   V, 145-153*
    1642-1658, W. Smith to Sir R.
    Leveson,   V, 172-173*

Letters of news—Of English or of general affairs—
Collections (cont.);
1642-1657, Sir W. Dugdale, V, 175-177*
1647, Sir P. Perceval to
Inchiquin, Egmont MSS., Vol. I, 357-437, passim*
1648(?)-1660, Hugh Potter, III, 86b-89b, passim*
1648-1660, Royalists in exile,
Bath MSS., Vol. II, 79-144, passim*
1649-1660, V, 144a-145b*
1650-1658, J. Wainwright (Parliamentary, etc.),
VI, 434b-444a*
1652-1659, to Col. Holles, III, 197a
1654-1660, J. Doddington to Sir R.
Leveson, V, 172b
1654-1658, Temple family, V, 171-172*
1658-1660, E. Gower to Sir R. Leveson,
V, 198b-199b*
1659-1660, VII, 461a-463a, passim*

Letters of news—Limited to a particular topic
(collections); see: entry under the topic,
e.g., Civil Wars, 1642-1651—History by year—
1648, newsletters of S. Kem; Parliamentary
affairs, newsletters, 16,18, 19 July, 1644.
Letters of news— Of English or of general affairs—
Single letters; 1604, July 19, court
news, VII, 668a
1604, Nov 10, 20, L. Bagot, IV, 338b
1613, Aug. 24, Sir E. Coke to Berkeley,
V, 345a-b

Letters of news—Of English or of general affairs—
　　Single letters (cont.);
1615, Feb. 14, J. Hunt to W. Bagot,　　IV, 334a*
1615, Oct. 23,　　　　　　　　　　　II, 87b*
1616,　　　　　　　　　　　　　　　II, 88a*
1616, Nov. 4,　　　　　　　　　　VII, 509a-b*
1617, July 7, Sir R. Winwood to C.
　Huygens,　　　　　　　　　　　III, 287b*
1618, June 23, T. Lorkin,

　　　　　　　　Bath MSS., Vol. II, 67-68*
1618, T. Lorkin,　　　　　　　　III, 195a
1619, Nov. 13, F. Bacon to Buckingham, III, 196b
1621, Feb. 20,　　　　　　　IV, 336b-337a*
1623, May 26, J. Finett(?) to Lord
　Clifford,　　　　　　　　　III, 39a-b*
1623, July 21, T. Lorkin,　　　III, 196b
1628(29), Mar. 6 and 1629, July, Sir H.
　Wotton,　　　III, 196b and Bath MSS., Vol. II, 74
1629, Sept. 3, Sir A. Forest to Sir R.
　Bevill,　　　　　　　　VIII(2), 50b*
1631, Dec. 13, E. Nicholas to
　Feilding,　　　　Denbigh MSS., Vol. V, 8-9*
1636, Apr. 5,　　　Denbigh MSS., Vol. V, 22*
1637, June 23,　　Denbigh MSS., Vol. V, 49-50*
1637, July 5, Sir H. Vane to Northumberland,
　　　　　　　　　　　　　　III, 74b*
1637, Aug. 24 and Sept. 20, H. Percy to
　Leicester,　　　　　　　III, 75a, b
1637, Oct. 13,　　Denbigh MSS., Vol. V, 51-52*

Letters of news—Of English or of general affairs—
    Single letters (cont.);
    1637, Oct. 18,   VIII(1), 552b*
    1639, Jan. 28, "English news" from
    The Hague, by E. Verney,   VII, 434b
    1639, Aug. 21, Sept. 12, 26,
    Northumberland to Leicester,   III, 77a, b*
    1639, Dec. 19, 26, Northumberland to
    Leicester,   III, 79a-b*
    1640, Apr. 27,   Denbigh MSS., Vol. V, 70*
    1640, Aug. 2, Archbishop Laud at Oatlands,
                          IX(2), 432a*
    1642, June 13, Sir T. Fairfax,   IX(2), 433a
    1644, after the Battle of Newbury,   I, 51a
    1647, Apr. 23,   IV, 274a
    1651, July 19, R. Hatter to B. Whitelocke,
                         III, 192a
    1653, Jan. 7, Sir C. Wolseley to Whitelocke
    in Sweden,   V, 313a
    1654, Jan. 24, W. Dobbins to J. Perceval,
               Egmont MSS., Vol. I, 534*
    1654, Mar. 28, Holland to Whitelocke about
    interview with Cromwell,   V, 313a
    1657, Oct. 22,   III, 254a
    1657, Nov. 17, S. Perceval from
    London,   Egmont MSS., Vol. I, 590-591*
    1658, Sept. 16,   V, 143b
    1659, Mar. 23, J. Howell, London,
                   IX(2), 444b-445a

Letters of news—Of English or of general affairs—
    Single letters (cont.);
    1659(60), Jan. 11,   XII(5), 6*
    1660, May 12,   V, 207*

Letters of news (single letters), limited to a
    particular topic; see: entry under the topic, e.g.
    La Rochelle, siege (etc.), newsletter, 11
    July, 1628.

Letters of news— Foreign (i.e. foreign affairs
    reported by Englishmen); temp. Jac. 1, from
    Italy,   VII, 516a
    1610, Feb. 22-1612, Dec. 1, Sir John
    Digby,   X(1), 520-617, passim*
    1614, May 30 (June 9); 1614, July 16(26);
        1621, May 9(24),   II, 51b, 52a, 59a
    1616, Dec. 28, Sir Didley Carleton from the
    Low Countries,   IX(2), 425a*
    1622, 1630, 1633, etc.,   I, 58a
    1623, June 23 - 1634, Sept. 9.   III, 285
    1623-1624,   III, 253b
    1624, Feb. 12, H. Conway,   III, 258b
    1625-1640,   XII(4), 471-527, passim*
    1625, May 15, from Earl of Oxford about
    attempt to relieve Breda,   V, 411a
    1625, Nov. 5, from "Cales," (Calais?),

                             III, 269a
    1626-1627,   XII(4), 471-483, passim*
    1628, Dec. 6 - 1632, May 25, to Lady

Letters of news—Foreign (i.e. foreign affairs reported
   by Englishmen) (cont.);
   Johanna Barrington,
                    VII, 537b-538a, 544a-548b, passim*
1631, Aug. 27-1638, Oct. 11, to
   Feilding,   VIII(1), 552-554*
1636, July 15(25)-1640(41), Feb. 5, to
   Feilding,   VI, 280-286*
1636(37), Feb. 15(25),
                    Denbigh MSS., Vol. V, 46-47*
1638, Oct., T. Denys to Sir W. Courtney, I, 51a
1639-1647 and later, from Constantinople,
   Leghorn, etc.,   VIII(3), 18b
1645, Sept. 8-1653, Mar. 12(22), Sir Ralph
   Verney,   VII, 451b-460a, passim*
1648-1660, Hyde, Holles and others,
                    Bath MSS., Vol. II, 79-144, passim*
1650, R. Bradshaw at Hamburg,   V, 426b-434b*
ca. 1652-1655, E. Hyde and others,   II, 82b
1656, July 16(26), W. Swyft at "Chaulny"
   to Whitelocke,   V, 313a
(1659), Nov. 13 from Algernon Sidney
   in Elsinore, to Whitelocke,   V, 314b

Letters patent; see: Monopolies.
Libels; by pamphleteers, temp. Car. 1,
                    IV, 354b (no. 174)
   cases in the Star Chamber; 1608-1618,
                    III, 55b, 57a, 58b, 59b; III, 64a-b*
—; against Mr. Talbot (Ireland),   IV, 374a

171

Lord's Supper; see: Communion.

Marches of Wales, Council of the (cont.);
  letters between Lords Presidents and
    county officers of Flint, 1618-1639,   IV, 355a

Markets; see: Fairs and markets.
Marque, letters of, against Irish rebels, 1641,
                             III, 84a-b
Marriage; gifts made to Earl of Somerset,
  1613,   II, 18a
  negotiations, settlements, etc.   III, 288b*;
     V, 389a-b*, 391b, 397a; V, 417a, 420a*; VIII(2), 64b
  legal aspects of, 1655, 1656,
               V, 394b-395a, 397b; VI, 447b
  of Sir G. Alington pronounced void,
  1631,   VII, 547a*
  of members of Perceval family,
       Egmont MSS., Vol. I, 125, 500-536, passim*;
           Vol. I, 569-578, 598, passim*
  to Roman Catholics, 1623,   IX(2), 367a
  abduction of a woman, in order to force
    marriage of her son with abductor's
    daughter, 1610,   V, 416b
Marriage, Royal; of Princess Elizabeth;
                   III, 281b; V, 408b
—; abatements on occasion of, 1613,
                   III, 204a; IV, 352b
—; collection of feudal aids on occasion
  of, 1612,   II, 86a; XII(4), 440
—; projected,   VII, 516a; X(1), 525-598, passim*
of Henrietta Maria,   IX(2), 427b*

Marriage, Royal (cont.);

    proposal of King of Poland for
       Princess Palatine, 1634,   VIII(3), 5b
    See also: Foreign relations—France; Spanish Match.

Marshes; sketch of Romney Marsh,   V, 407a
    annuity from marshland, 1623,   V, 410b
    salt marshes claimed for King, 1637,   XI(7), 98*
    See also: Fen drainage.

Masques; temp. Jac. 1,   III, 281b; V, 355a*
    Inner Temple masque,   IX(2), 386b
Master of Ceremonies, bill of, for attendance
    of ambassadors, 1626,   IX(2), 428a

Masters of Requests; see: Requests, Masters of.
Masters of Chancery; see: Chancery, Masters of.
Maypole; at Guildford, temp. Jac. 1,

                        VII, 668a, 675b*
    fines for cutting of, 1637,   IX(2), 496a*
Mead; see: Metheglin.
Measures; see: Weights and measures.
Medical affairs;   II, 63b;
          Rutland MSS., Vol. IV, 454-540, passim*
    College of Physicians' disciplinary action
      against a surgeon, 1605,   III, 53a*
    Northumberland's expenses for illness,
      1603-1615,   VI, 228b-231a*
    appearance of the body of an "illustrious prince"
      after death,   VII, 675a
    Spa at Rowley, 1626,   VII, 543b

Medical affairs (cont.);

    small-pox, London, 1638,   IX(2), 497a*

    sickness at Pontefract, 1645,   VI, 329b*

    bill for curing wound, 1646,   IX(2), 393a*

    leper to be paid 20s. by County Treasurer of

        Northants, 1660,   V, 403b

    advice and prescriptions; II, 46b; III, 121b; IV, 348b;

      V, 365a, 366a; VI, 462b; VIII(2), 29a, 51a; VIII(3), 19b;

         IX(2), 375b; XII(4), 426; XII(4), 440-441, 484, 485*;

                        Egmont MSS., Vol. I, 277*

    —; lady "to be well advised before she use the

        Bath...in hir way heather,"   VIII(2), 56b

    —; "Eyebright" for the eye,   IV, 329a

    —; for the stone,   III, 196b

    —; from Sir T. Browne on strangury, III, 272b

    See also: Apothecaries; Drugs; Hospitals;

      King's evil; Physicians and surgeons; Plague.

Memoirs, personal; see: Diaries, journals

    and memoirs.

Mercers' Company, its action about Northampton's

    charities, 1629,   V, 412b

Merchant Adventurers; relations with Netherlands,

    1613,   III, 212a

    rivalry of two Companies, 1615,

            III, 196b and Bath MSS., Vol. II, 63-64*

    complaint of, against Middelburg, 1620, II, 57b

    papers about, 1621, etc.,   III, 190b, 191a

    petitions by, 1640-1642(?),   III, 191b

    letters to T. Pengelly, 1650(?)-

Merchant Adventurers (cont.);

1660(?),   VII, 691b

   bill for "liberty of trade," as concerning,   II, 18b

Merchant Taylors Hall, great supper at,

   (1604),   VII, 526b

Merchants; papers relating to the Staple,

     temp. Car. 1,   III, 191a

  desiring to continue to try foreign contracts

   by civil law,   V, 433a

  English; at Bilbao, 1647,   II, 78b

  —; in Holland, 1643,   III, 196b

  —; in Poland, letter on behalf of, 1627,

                                 IV, 411a

  —; in service of Venice, 1647,

                   Bath MSS., Vol. II, 79*

  —; injuries to, by officers of Inquisition,

   1608,   VI, 351b

  —; Companies to maintain forty-five sail

   for convoy, Feb., 1655,   VI, 439b

Merchants Strangers, case of the, in Star

    Chamber, 1619,   II, 3b, II, 56b

Metheglin, recipe for,   XII(4), 526*

Military affairs; temp. Jac. 1,   II, 46a (no. clxxx)

  answer of Prince Henry to propositions

  concerning, temp. Jac. 1,   VII, 515a

  See also: Army and militia; Bishops' War(s);

  Civil Wars; Defense; Garrisons; Ordnance;

  Palatinate.

Military art and science;

III, 54b, 119a; IX(2), 371b (no. 708)

indefensibility of Romney Marsh in invasion,

V, 407a

Militia (trained bands); see: Army and militia.

Minerals; assay of,   XII(5), 6

See also: Gold.

Mines and mining; 1617(18)-1621.   VI, 223a

See also: Lead.

Ministers; see: Clergy (or ministers).

Ministers, Committee for Ejecting Scandalous; see:

Scandalous Ministers, Committee for Ejecting.

Ministers, Committee for Plundered; see:

Plundered Ministers, Committee for.

Mint, the; temp. Jac. 1,   VI, 312a

King's seizure of money in, 1640,   III, 81b-82a*

officers, expenses, "engines," assays, etc.,

VIII(1), 61a, 66a, b, 69b, 70a, 95a

coinage for Ireland, 1602,   VI, 311b

See also: Coin.

Money; see: Coin; Trade.

Monopolies; licenses, etc., for, temp.

Jac. 1(?),   III, 66b; V, 355a; VI, 311b

grievances of House of Commons regarding,

IX(2), 366a

Statute of,   VIII(2), 50a

for sole making of bills and entries of imports,

temp. Jac. 1,   VII, 576b

for making rape seed oil, 1626,   V, 358b

Monopolies (cont.);

Murderers (cont.);

    warning to intercept escaped murderer
      at Chester, 1621,   VI, 472a

Music lecture, 1642,   II, 78b

Musical instruments; the polyphon, 1655,   XII(5), 5*
    "chest of viols" not for sale at Ł10, 1622,

                                   VII, 530a

Musicians; annuities for four, 1612,   II, 79a
    of Prince of Wales, at Ł 40 a year, 1611,

                                   VII, 670a

    organist of Windsor Chapel,   VIII(1), 7b, 10a*

Musters; see: Army and militia—Musters;
    Array, Commissioners of.

Naval and maritime affairs; "exposition of . . .
    a ship and . . . navigation,"   VI, 304b
    actions against Spain, etc.,   VI, 307a
    recommendations for defense,   VI, 305a
    temp. Jac. 1,   II, 46a (no. clxxx)
    temp. Jac. 1 - Car. 1, including navy under
    Nottingham and under Northumberland,

                    III, 71b-76b, passim, 84a;
          VI, 303b-305a, passim, 313b-314b, passim

    temp. Car. 1(?), arming of a fleet with
    assistance of King of Spain,   V, 312b
    supplies,   III, 76a, 79a, 186a, 190b, 265a;
           VI, 304b, 314a, 351b; VIII(1), 98b-99a*

    1615, Jan. 9, English ship seized by
    Governor of Dieppe,   III, 38b

Naval and maritime affairs (cont.);

Naval and maritime affairs (cont.);

Naval and maritime affairs; See also (cont.);
    1655-1659.

Negroes taken to Virginia and Bermuda,
    1619-1621,   VIII(2), 31-37, passim*

Netherlands, War with; see: War with the
    Dutch.

New Year's gifts; satirical proposal to
    "sequester,"   V, 414a
    from Royal Jewel-House, 1617-1640,
                      VII, 594a-b, passim

Newsletters; see: Letters of news.

Nobility; list of,   I, 54b; III, 63a, 86a;
                IX(2), 371b-372a, 388a
    precedency of,   VI, 459b
    conference on trials of peers and
      peeresses for treason,   I, 12b
    peers created by James I,   IV, 341a, VII, 526b*
    petition from, relating to new titles,
      1620,   XII(4), 457
    to wear mourning for James I, 1625,   V, 411a*
    adherents of Charles I among, 1639,
      1640, etc.,   III, 294a
    sums levied for subsidy on,   V, 411a
    list of Royalist,   IV, 408b
    See also: Baronage; Baronetcies; Baronets;
      Establishment, the; Peerage.

Non-conformists; imprisoned; (1632),   VII, 548a*
    See also: Sects.

North, Council of the; see: Council of the North.

Oastmen; see: Coal trade.

Oath; to be taken by Commissioners of Ecclesiastical
    Causes, 1611,   III, 58a

    against change in Church government,
        1640,   I, 13a; VII, 433b; VIII(2), 57b

    of allegiance; 1604,   VII, 516b

    —; Pope Paul's bulls about, 1606,   IV, 372a

    —; not required of those leaving for service
      with Spain, (1621),   VIII(3), 5b

    of supremacy; to be taken by all royal servants
      and all who travel or come from abroad,
      1605,   VII, 526b*

    —; letter of G. Blackwell, archpriest,
      regarding, 1606,   IX(2), 366b

    —; letter of Cardinal Bellarmino to G. Blackwell
      regarding, 1607,   IX(2), 367a

    See also: Bishops' War, First; Privy
    Council; Recusants.

Oats, price of, 1637,   VI, 231b

Offices, applications for (mainly to Buckingham);
    appointments, etc., to, 1618-1625,
                          II, 53a-62b, passim

Offices, Book of; see: Establishment, the.

Offices, Inquiry of Commissioners into exacted
    fees and innovated; 1623,   III, 213b

    temp. Car. 1,   III, 69a*, 70b, 71b

Officials—Royal and State; list of holders of
    "a certain office,"   VII, 592b

Officials—Royal and State (cont.);

Order of the Garter (cont.);

    Jac. 1,   VII, 529b, 670a, b, 674a-676a, passim

    given to the King of Sweden, 1627,   IV, 411a;

                         V, 304b; VII, 233b

    Chancellor of,   VII, 673b, 674a, 678a

    Keeper of the Wardrobe to furnish velvet

      and taffeta to lords for Garter robes,

      1607,   V, 408a

    Jewel-House lends plate to Knights for

      their installation, 1606,   VII, 593b-594a

    King's installation, 1625,   VIII(3), 5b

Ordnance; temp. Jac. 1,   IV, 371b; VI, 334b

    temp. Car. 1,   I, 43b; III, 76b, 191b

    accounts, 1606, 1612,   VI, 322b-323a

    table of weight, powder, shot, etc., for

      different cannon,   VII, 682b

Ordnance General, office of,   III, 213b

Ore; see: Lead; Mines and mining.

Painter of emblems (J. Starkey), assistance

    asked for him for journey to Holland,   V, 368b

Paintings; see: Pictures.

Palaces; grant of land in purlieus of Whitehall and

    Westminster, 12 Mar., 1604,   V, 407a-b

    North Park of Hampton Court,   VI, 323a

Palatinate; letters, etc., relating to,

    1619-1637,

        III, 285a-b; VII, 576b; VIII(3), 9b (no. 7), 14a (no. 60)

    money raised for, (Bohemian loan),

Palatinate (cont.);

1619-1622,   II, 88a; VI, 461a; VIII (1), 2a*;

                                  IX (2), 368b-369a

letter of Council of the Palatinate to

  Digby, 21 Sept., 1621,   VIII (1), 214a

estimate for war, by Privy Council,

  1620,   III, 212b

James I and, 1622-1623,   VIII (1), 94b (no. 7);

                    VIII (1), 214a-215b, passim*

newsletter, 1621,   IV, 336b-337a*

Mansfeld's actions, Sept., 1621,   II, 59b

petition of Commons about aid for, 1621,   III, 65a

proposed suspension of arms in,

  1622 (?),   III, 212a; VII, 674b

speech of the Houses to the King on treaty

  regarding, 1623 (24),   III, 67a

musters ordered for, 1624,   II, 87b

speech about restitution of, 1624,   IV, 359b

appointment of Buckingham as commander

  of fleet and forces for, 1628,   III, 70a

correspondence of Feilding about,

  1636-1638,   Denbigh MSS., Vol. V, p. 19ff, passim*

See also: Foreign relations; Spanish Match.

Papists; see: Recusants; Roman Catholics.

Parishes; see: Churches.

Parks and chases; keepership of Farnham, co.

  Surrey, temp. Jac. 1,   VII, 669a, 675a*

deer in Guildford Park to be "viewed,"

  1608,   VII, 668b-669a

Parks and chases (cont.);

    keepership and office of "palister" of

      North Park of Hampton Court, 1622,   VI, 323a

    Hatfield Chase or Forest sequestered from

      Lord and Lady Morley to Sir T.

      Barrington, 1644,   VII, 569b*

    grant to G. Hervie to run 12 horses in

      Havering Park, 1614,   VII, 593b

    repairing rails in Henley Park, 1609,   VII, 669b

    disbursements for Hyde Park,

      1611-1612,   IX (2), 424b-425a*

    payment for timber in Great Park of

      Stanstead, 1609,   VII, 669b

    keeper of one of Bishop of Winchester's

      parks, 1605,   VII, 668a

    charge for draining the Great Park of

      Windsor, 1623,   IX (2), 426a

Parliament; roll of Barons of, 10 Jac. 1,   VI, 459b

    Bishop of Bangor exempted from attendance

      at, 9 Mar., 1614,   V, 417a

    at Oxford; 1644,   I, 54b (no. 14)

    —; resolutions,   III, 86a

    Committees of (in the Civil Wars); see:

      Civil Wars.

    summons to, by Cromwell, 1653,   III, 216b

    salaries of officers of, 1654,   VIII (3), 6a

    House of Commons; list of members,

      1614,   VIII (2), 28b-29a

    —; burghership of Retford transferred,

Parliament; House of Commons (cont.);

Parliamentary affairs (i.e. unofficial material)
  (cont.);

letter of the King, 11 Dec., 1621,   VI, 351b
Salisbury to James I on calling
  Parliament, (n.d.),   III, 214b
letter and remonstrance to Charles I,   III, 120b
repayment to Sergeant-at-Arms of expenses
  for House of Commons, 1625,   IX(2), 426b
arguments for Parliament granting
  liberal supplies, Aug., 1625,   V, 411a
Heneage Finch tries to escape Speakership,
  1625-1626,   Finch MSS., Vol. I, 43ff*
letter of former M.P. to Commons,
  ca. 1627,   III, 214b
newsletter, 23 Apr., 1628,   III, 69b
disputes with King, 1639(?),   IX(2), 343b
rumors and news of, 8 Dec., 1639-
  17 Feb., 1640,   IX(2), 498-499, passim*
newsletter, 13-21 Apr., 1640,   XI(7), 98*
petition of ten lords for summoning
  Parliament, 1640,   V, 214a
petition to King to summon Parliament,
  1640,   VIII(2), 57a
letter of Sir J. Dryden, 26 Nov., 1640,
       II, 63b*
plot for bringing up army against
  Parliament, May, 1641,   III, 84a
report of Pym's "heads of agreement,"
  etc., Aug., 1641,   III, 84a

Parliamentary affairs (i.e. unofficial material)
(cont.);

Parliamentary affairs (i.e. unofficial material)
(cont.);

Parliamentary proceedings—1604-1614; (cont.);

petitions to House of Commons, temp.

See also: Impositions; Revenue; Scotland;

Spanish Match.

Parliamentary proceedings—1621-10 Jan., 1642;

Parliamentary proceedings—1621-10 Jan., 1642
(cont.);

For Parliamentary proceedings of this period
in print; see: Appendix A.

Parliamentary proceedings—Temp. Car. 1 or

10 Jan., 1642-1649;   I, 31a
petitions to Parliament,   VII, 687a-b*
addresses of Commons to King, temp.
Car. 1,   I, 61a
speeches in Commons, temp. Car. 1,   I, 61a
orders of Commons, 1641-1648,   III, 191b
28 Mar. -4 June, 1642,   I, 63a
25 Apr. -2 May, 1642,   VII, 677b
narration by a member, 6 May, 1642,

III, 84b-85a*

Lord Wharton on votes in Parliament on
affairs in Ireland, 6, 23 Apr., 1647,

IV, 274a-b*

Covenant taken by the Lords, 15 Oct.,
1643,   V, 313b
list of Independents in Commons,

Egmont MSS., Vol. I, 440-441*

Parliamentary proceedings— 1649-1660; report of
Committee appointed to revise Statutes,
1650,   III, 192a
Committee for Regulating the Universities,
1651,   VIII(2), 64a
appointment of Cromwell as Protector,
1653,   I, 45a

Parliamentary proceedings — 1649-1660 (cont.);

   Broghill's speech against "bill of extraordinary

    taxes,"   VII, 678b

   candidacy of W. Dobbins for Irish

    vacancy, 1657,   Egmont MSS. , Vol. I, 593*

   letter regarding proceedings, 1659,   III, 269a

   notes in House of Commons, 1659,   IX(2), 396a

   See also: East India Company (English).

Pasture; see: Inclosures.

Patents of inventions; see: Inventions.

Peace, Justices of the; see: Justices of the Peace.

Pedlars, licensing of, 1617,   III, 286b

Peerage; proceedings in claims,   II, 46b

   warrants for patents of, temp. Car. 1,   I, 34b

   See also: Baronage; Baronetcies;

    Baronets; Nobility.

Peers and peeresses, conference about trials

    of, for treason,   I, 12b

Peers, Council of, at York, 1640; see: York,

    Council of Peers at, 1640.

Penmanship, copy-book for J. Hampden, 1610,

                          III, 253b

Pensions; to individuals, 1607,   III, 264b

   1626,   VII, 676b

   1651,   IX(2), 441b (29 Apr.)

   proceedings of Commissioners for,

    1656-1657,   III, 212b

   for soldiers; garrison of Berwick, 1640,

                         III, 265b

Pensions; for soldiers (cont.);

—; disability allowance for lieutenant,
1648, III, 288b
Petitions (collections of); 1621-1628(?),

III, 204b-205a
1631-1639, III, 191b
1649-1650, addressed to B. Whitelocke,

III, 192a
See also: Parliamentary affairs; Parliamentary
proceedings.
Pewter, bought by the Chamber of Marlborough,
1615, IV, 351b (no. 108)
Physicians and surgeons, fees etc., VII, 434b;
IX (2), 425b (1 Oct., 1618)*;
Rutland MSS., Vol. IV, 454-522, passim*
Pictures; Rutland MSS., Vol. IV, 462-540, passim*
imported by Lord Arundell, 1636 (37),

VIII (1), 554a*
directions for purchase and transportation
of Delanave collection for Charles I,
1637, IV, 258a-b*
to be removed from churches, 1642, V, 350b
by Lely, 1654, VI, 437b
a Rubens presented to Duke of Buckingham,

VIII (3), 10a (no. 18)
portrait; of Sir T. Fairfax by "Mr.
Corell," servant of Vandyke, 1646, VI, 466a
—; of young Perceval, 1650,

Egmont MSS., Vol. I, 491-492*

196

Pictures; portrait (cont.);

—; of Countess of Sussex, 1640,   VII, 434b

portraits of members of Wroth family,
1650, 1651,   VI, 347a

Pirates; Sir R. Hawkins charged with
favoring, 1609,   III, 56b

admiral appointed for suppression of,
1620,   III, 64b

petition of ship charged with piracy,
1616,   III, 286a-b

case in Star Chamber against three
merchant ships, 1612,   III, 59b

ships to guard Iceland and North Sea
(fishing) fleet against, 1626,   VII, 530b*

fear of, in Mediterranean, 1645,   VII, 452a

protected by King of Denmark, 1650,

VI, 430b, 434a

captures of English ships by, 1659,

Egmont MSS., Vol. I, 602*

Algerine (Turkish); ransom from,   IX(2), 386b

—; charge to Hythe for suppressing,
1620,   II, 92a

—; expedition against, 1621,   II, 59a (no. 360)

—; letters about, Sept., 1636,   III, 73b

—; advice of a seaman about, temp.
Car. 1,   III, 211b

—; danger from, off British coasts, temp.
Car. 1,   Egmont MSS., Vol. I, 90, 120*

—; plans for suppressing, Jan.,

Pirates; (cont.);

West Indies, 1619-1623,   VIII(2), 35a, 36b, 39a*
See also: Dunkirkers.

Plague; 1608,   VII, 669a, b
   1630,   VII, 546a
   1636,   III, 116b
   1638,   IX(2), 497a-b*
   1640,   IX(2), 432a*
   in co. Lincoln, 1625,   XII(4), 473
   in London,   VII, 529a
   —; 1603,   VII, 667b
   —; 1625,   VI, 335a
   —; 1626,   III, 43a
   —; 1636,   III, 191b
   —; 1637,   V, 312a; VI, 329a
   in the Navy, (1605),   VII, 526b
   in Shropshire, letter of Bridgewater
    about, 1631,   III, 258b
   at Chester, 1647-1648,   V, 339b
   at Newcastle, 1625,   III, 39b
   at Shrewsbury, 1650,   V, 342b-343a
Plate; list of, for Jesus College,   II, 64a
   —; of Sir J. Fortescue, 1608,   XII(4), 409*
   —; of Pierrepont family,   IX(2), 375b
   delivered to E. Home, 1633,   V, 362b
   coined into money, 1643,   II, 48b
   brought from Spain for coining, 1636,   III, 73a-b*
   seized from Sir R. Graham, 1646,   VI, 323a
   order to pay goldsmith for, 1647,   III, 288b

199

Plate (cont.);

    bound for Ireland, seized, 1655,

                Egmont MSS., Vol. I, 563, 566-567*

  See also: Coin; Gold; Jewel-House;

    Mint, the.

Plays and players; payments for, 1616(?),   IV, 327a

  1623, 1624,   IV, 327b

  sentences of Star Chamber against;

    1610,   III, 57b

  —; 1614,   III, 62b-63a

  costume, 1617,   II, 47a

  punishments for stage play on Sabbath

    day, 1610,   III, 57b

  See also: Masque.

Plots; supposed, 1642, letter from the Gate

  House about,   VIII(2), 58a*

  Royalist, 1657-1660,

              Bath MSS., Vol. II, 117-142, passim*

  intended insurrection, 1655,   II, 87b

Plundered Ministers, Committee for; actions

  of, in Bedfordshire, 1644,   VIII(1), 5b

  payment on order of; to a Rochester

    minister, 1650,   VI, 473a

  —; to an Essex minister, 1652,   VI, 473a

  See also: Sequestrations; Tithes.

Pluralities; dispensations for, temp. Car.

    1,   I, 34a

  rectories granted to King's chaplain, VI, 472b

Poaching; see: Hunting.

Poursuivant-at-arms (cont.);

 of,   VI, 459b

Preachers, Commissioners for Approving

 Public, 1656,   III, 287b

Preachers, for commemoration at Trinity

 College, Cambridge, (1641),   VII, 577a*

Preaching; 1622,   II, 61a

 Archbishop of Canterbury to bishops on,

 1622,   V, 410a; VIII(1), 2b

 subscriptions for Archbishop of Armagh

 to preach at St. Paul's, 1641, 1642,

            VII, 435b, 443b

 by a lieutenant near Bristol, 1645,   IV, 273a

 by S. Oates, "schismatic" (Anabaptist),

 1646,   V, 390b, 397a

Prerogative, royal, letter of James I about,

 1621,   XII(4), 463

Presbyterians, Minutes of Westminster

 Assembly, 1643-1652,   III, 368a

Prices; 1603-1658,

    Rutland MSS., Vol. IV, 447-541, passim*

 complaints of high prices; temp. Jac. 1(?),

             IV, 331a

 —; 1622,   IV, 343a

 on commodities, 1646,

      Egmont MSS., Vol. I, 345-347*

 of household goods and livestock of H. and O.

 ap Robert, 1618,   V, 417b

 paid to joiner, 1631,   V, 418b

Prices (cont.);

    of bricks, 1652,   VII, 458a

    of cochineal (worth weight in silver),

      1659,   VII, 461b

    of sheep for King's Household, 1635,   V, 402a

    of iron, ca. 1609,   VI, 449b

    of horses, oats and beds for Parliamentary

      army,   V, 403a

    of horses for King's stud, 1612,   VI, 471b*

    of fruit trees, 1653,   Egmont MSS., Vol. I, 531*

    See also: Accounts (receipts and expenses) —

    Private; Accounts (receipts and expenses) —Public;

    Agriculture; Clothing and dress; Food and drink;

    Household, Royal; Household accounts; Household

    goods; Houses; Jewelry; Land; Landed estates; Textile

    fabrics; Tin; Wine; Wool.

Priests, repression of, temp. Jac. 1

    or Car. 1,   III, 212a

Printer; (J. Barnes), assistance asked

    for journey to Holland by,   V, 368a

    widow of a, to carry on tavern at Oxford,

    1624,   V, 368b

Printing; request of Stationers' Company to control,

    1637,   III, 75b

    See also: Books; Libels.

Prisoners; see: Civil Wars; Jails and prisons.

Prisons; see: Jails and prisons.

Privateer arrested on complaint of French

Privateer (cont.);

    merchants, 1646,   IX(2), 428b

Privy Chamber, Groom of the; see: Groom of
    the Privy Chamber.

Privy Council; 16th to 17th cent.;   I, 61a

    —; temp. Jac. 1,   IV, 330-331; VI, 312b

    —; temp. Jac. 1-Car. 1, I, 57-58, passim, III, 281a

    orders for attendants on lords dining
        in Council chamber,   VII, 592a

    resolutions regarding grievances of House
        of Commons, in respect to monopolies,

                          IX(2), 366a

    letters of, about Chester,   III, 211a

    diet books, 1602, 1605, 1635,   IX(2), 413a

    rules of James I for attendance in,   VIII(2), 29b

    order of, for payment of subsidy of 43
        Eliz., 1604,   VI, 223b

    letter on reformation of alehouses,
        1607,   VII, 668b

    form of oath in, 1623,   III, 285a

    orders to be observed in assemblies
        of, Feb., 1627(28),   III, 69b

    oath taken by members of; (1640?),   III, 83b

    —; 1643,   III, 285a

Privy seal, custody of,   VIII(3), 20a (no. 3)

Privy seals; see: Benevolences and loans to the
    King; Revenue.

Prizes taken at sea; Spanish ships; 1605,

                          VI, 311a

Puritans (cont.);

See also: Churches.

Purveyance of provision for Royal Household;

    see: Household, Royal.

Quakers,   VI, 441a-b*; VII, 687a

Quarries, in Forest of Shotover and

    Stowood, 1637,   VIII(3), 12b (no. 34)

Racing; see: Horse racing.

Raffle, 1612,   Bath MSS., Vol. II, 61-62*

Rape seed oil, patent for, 1626,   V, 358b

Recusants; papers about; temp. Jac. 1-

    Car. 1,   I, 46b;

                 II, 59b; III, 38a, 39b; III, 60b*, 190b;

                 V, 300b, 312a; VII, 676a; VIII(1), 27b

—; in Yorkshire, 1608,   III, 299a

gratitude expressed to Prince by,

    temp. Jac. 1,   VII, 516a

commissions concerning; 1620,   VIII(2), 29a

—; in co. Derby, Mar., 1606(07),   XII(4), 404

—; in Lindsey, 1624,   XII(4), 471*

commissions for compounding with,

    temp. Jac. 1 and Car. 1,   I, 34a

writs served against, 1627,   XII(4), 481

fines on; 1610,   III, 57b

—; members of Throckmorton family,

    1635,   X(4), 171

imprisoned, for refusing to take religious

    oath; 1605(?),   III, 53a

Revenue (cont.);

wages, fees and pensions of officers of,
1628, III, 265a-b
of Duchy of Cornwall, 1633-1634,
VIII(3), 12a(no. 19)
King's seizure of money in the Mint,
1640, III, 81b-82a*
"for Commonwealth," V, 314a
accounts of Receiver of Revenues of
(the late) Charles I, 1650, V, 403b
for England, Scotland and Ireland, 1654, VII, 687a
See also: Aids, feudal; Assessments,
rates, etc.; Benevolences and loans to
the King; Civil Wars; Customs duties;
Fines; Impositions; Loan; Loans; Ship
money; Subsidies; Taxation; Tithes.
Revenue, Committee for, their request for
arrears of rent, 1646, VIII(2), 63a

Rhé expedition; see: La Rochelle.
Ripon, Treaty of, 1640; see: Bishops' War,
Second,
Rivers; Avon, improvements, ca. 1617, I, 57a
Kefney (Cefni?), diversion of, 1636, V, 419a
New River, to be brought into London, III, 58a*
Ouse, navigation of, temp. Car. 1(?),
VIII(2), 63b(no. 609)
Thames, gravel and sand from, 1633, III, 191a
river between Surrey and Sussex turned
from its course, 1616, VII, 672b

213

Royalists abroad; correspondence,   IV, 274b-275a*
Col. G. Holles, 1648-1660,

       Bath MSS., Vol. II, 79-80, 99-145*
Sir E. Hyde, 1649-1660, III, 195b and Bath MSS.,

       Vol. II, 80-145*; IX(2), 440a*
Sir R. Verney, 1643-1653,   VII, 445a-459b*
George Digby, 2d Earl of Bristol, 1646-

  1662, |VIII(1), 27b-30b, passim*, 217b-219a
plots of, 1648,   VIII(1), 552b-553a*
activities of Rochester on behalf of

  Charles II, 1652-1654,   V, 314b
appeal of Jermyn to Mazarin for aid in

  restoring King, 24 Aug., 1659,   IX(2), 409b
passes to Winchelsea to travel,

      Finch MSS., Vol. I, 58-59, 75
See also: Delinquents; Foreign service.

Sabbath day, punishments for stage play
  on, 1610,   III, 57b
Sailors; see: Seamen.
Salaries; of musicians of Prince of Wales,
  1611,   VII, 670a
of officers of Parliament and others,
  1654,   VII(3), 6a
of Lord Chief Justice of Upper
  Bench, 1649,   III, 266a
of clergyman at Halstead, 1643,   VII, 550a
See also: Fees; Household, Royal; Wages.

"Sallee" pirates; see: Pirates.

Salt marshes, argument that they are the
    King's, 1637,   XI(7), 98
Salt trade; 1603-1605,   VI, 222b-223a, 311a
    salt process; 1626,   VIII(2), 50a
    —; 1637,   IX(2), 369b (no. 15)

Saltpetre;   III, 190b; V, 355b; VI, 311b; VII, 515b
    proclamation about right to open works,
        1634,   XI(7), 97*
    plan for making, 1637(?),   III, 75b
    See also: Gunpowder.

Sassafras, wine to be made from, in
    Virginia, 1620,   V, 341a
Scandalous Ministers, Committee for Ejecting,
    appointments to, 1657,   IX(2), 395b-396a*

Scholarship; see: Learning and Scholarship.
Schooling and diet of boys, account for,
    1646,   Egmont MSS., Vol. I, 300*

Schoolmaster, correspondence about a,
    1617,   IV, 327a
Schools; Charterhouse (Sutton Hospital);
    suit against, 1612,   III, 187a
    —; petition of Master of, 1628(?),   III, 286b
    —; Bacon's opinion to King James on
    "imployment of,"   III, 215b
    —; Cromwell appointed Governor of,
    1650,   VIII(2), 64a
    —; Committee of Parliament for (Sutton
    Hospital), 1650,   VIII(2), 64a

Schools (cont.);

Scotland; proposed union with (cont.);

  temp. Jac. 1,

                    I, 48a (P. 150, 151); II, 46a (no. clxxvi)
— ; speech of King in Parliament
House, Edinburgh, on, 17 June, 1617,

                                        IX (2), 386b
Commissioners for, "make an end," (n. d.):

                                        VII, 529a
relations with; 1639-1640,

                    II, 7b; VI, 457b; VIII (2), 56a*
— ; speeches about "antenati and postnati,"
  temp. Jac. 1,   VII, 516b
episcopacy in, 1637-1640,

                    III, 79b, 83b; IV, 374a; VI, 352b
trade with, demands of Scottish Commissioners
  concerning, 1641,   III, 84a
See also: Bishops' War (s); Civil Wars;
  Covenant, Solemn League and.
Scots, grants of crown lands to,   V, 323b
Scriveners, proclamation against,
  1621,   II, 59b (no. 377)
Seamen; allowance to,   VI, 314a
  to be restored to Portsmouth from
  Kingston, 1626,   VII, 676a
  plan for compulsory contribution
  for the disabled from, 1639,   III, 79b*
  withholding of their wages, 1640,   VI, 285-286*
  relief of maimed, 1651,   V, 403b
  Monck's orders for care of, 5 Aug., 1653,
                                        IX (2), 442b
                    217

Sequestrations; of estates (cont.);

—; of Earl of Cumberland, 1650-1651,   III, 41a
—; of Mrs. Edwards, 1652,   II, 67b
—; of Sir J. Gell, 21 Mar., 1652-   ,

IX(2), 395a-b, 396a-b*

—; of Sir R. Graham, 1644-1648,   VI, 323a
—; of Lord and Lady Morley, to Sir

Thomas Barrington, 1644,   VII, 569b*

—; of Mr. Muce, 1644,   IV, 267a
—; of Earl of Northumberland (attempts

to sequestrate), 1650(?),   III, 87a-b*

—; of Sir P. Perceval in Somerset,

1650,   Egmont MSS., Vol. I, 494-498*

—; of R. Puleston, 1659,   II, 67b-68a
—; of Sir T. Russell, 1649,   VIII(3), 11b
—; of Thomas Russell of Little

Malvern, 1649,   II, 73a

—; of Sir R. Strickland, 1646,   V, 331b
—; of Sir R. Verney (discharged), 1647,

VII, 460b

—; of Sir G. Villiers, 1645,   IV, 273a
—; of R. Williams of Derby, 1644, IX(2), 392a-b
in Bedfordshire, 1644, 1650,

VIII(1), 3a-7a, passim*, 11a

in Dorset, proceedings of Parliamentary

Committee, 1646-1650,   VIII(1), 210b

in Essex, 1645, 1646,   VIII(3), 10a
of vicarage of Kirkby Lonsdale,

1646,   VII, 686b-687a

Sequestrations (cont.);

    of Lordship of Padmore (not to be
      sequestered), 1644,   IV, 267a

    of church of "Pleskie," (Pleshey),
      Essex, 1643,   VII, 549b

    rents of Canons of Windsor, 1645,

                VIII(1), 7b, 10a*

    See also: Delinquents; Roman Catholics.

Sergeant ancient, appointment with
    fee, 1634,   III, 265b

Sergeant-at-arms; allowance of E. Birkhead
    as, 1652,   III, 288b

    expenses for House of Commons to be
    repaid to, 1625,   IX(2), 426b

Servants; wages and payments to, 1603-
    1616,   VI, 228-231, passim, 323b-324a*, 327b, 450a

    list of Northampton's,   V, 408b

    in Virginia; temp. Jac. 1,   V, 341a

    —; 1616-1629,   VIII(2), 31-48, passim*

    a "gentle serving woman," 1608,   VIII(1), 283b

    livery of coach-pages, 1652,   VII, 458b-459a*

    See also: Household, Royal.

Sewers; laborers to scour and cleanse
    "Milnedyke," 1615,   VI, 423b

    fines set by Commissioners of, 1621,   VII, 576b

Sheep; prices of, 1601-1608,   IV, 414a

    for Royal Household, with prices,
    temp. Car. 1,   V, 401b-402a

Ships (cont.);

Ships (cont.);

Spanish Match; letters and papers about (cont.);

VIII(3), 22b (no. 88)

—; of J. Wadsworth from Spain,   III, 282a

—; of Winwood (or Wm. Wood),   IV, 354b (no. 176)

articles of agreement for,   V, 355b, 410b

proceedings about, in Parliament;

I, 43b; IV, 353b, 374a

—; King's speech, on breaking it off,   III, 66b

—; Buckingham's speech,   III, 66b; IV, 359b

papal correspondence about; with James I,

IV, 373b

—; with Prince Charles,

I, 54b (no. 8); II, 43b; III, 185a;

IV, 355a; V, 410b; XII(4), 469

—; with Archbishop of Conches,   III, 185a

journey of Prince and Buckingham to

   Spain;   V, 410b;

VII, 509a; VIII(1), 2b

—; list of attendants for,   III, 284b*

—; horses, attendants, etc., brought to Spain

   by T. Wilbram,   VI, 334b*

— ; letter of Prince to King of Spain,

III, 66a-b*

—; news of conclusion of articles,

Bath MSS., Vol. II, 71-72*

—; letter of Conway to Buckingham in

   Spain,   III, 265a*

—; Prince's gifts at leaving,   III, 196b*

Stationery, supplied to Secretary of
    State, 1637,   VI, 472a

Statues, account for those bought of
    contractors for the late King's goods,
                                   IX(2), 444b*
Steel, patent for, to Dr. Fludd, 1622,   II, 60b
Steward; appointment of deputy steward
    of the "late monastery of Furness,"
    1607,   III, 247a
    recommendation of former student for,
    1625,   XII(4), 475

Students; see: Schools; Universities.
Subsidies; of James I; in co. Cumberland,
    1625,   III, 39b
    —; in co. Derby,   XII(4), 402-404, 410
    —; in Essex, 1608,   VII, 543b
    —; in co. Lincoln,   XII(4), 462, 463
    —; in co. Rutland, 1624,   V, 401b
    —; in Surrey, 1621,   VII, 674b
    of Charles I;   III, 40b; VII, 676b; XII(4), 483ff
    —; from Hundred of Kerrier,   IV, 405a
    —; in Keythorpe and Goadby, 1642,   V, 387b
    —; in Lancashire, Mar., 1640,   V, 344a
    —; in co. Northampton, 1628,   V, 401b
    —; in co. Rutland, 1628,   V, 401b
    1643, 1644, from London,   II, 73b
    on lords and ladies,   V, 411a
    for gentlemen pensioners, 1625,   IX(2), 426b

Subsidies (cont.);

    due from Lord Rich, 1603-1611,   VIII(2), 28a-b

    paid by Northumberland, 1609,   VI, 229a

    due from Earl of Warwick, 1631,   VIII(2), 50b

    Commissioners for Revision of

      Subsidies, 1603,   XII(4), 394

    payment asked for by Council on

      subsidy of 43 Eliz., 1604,   VI, 223b

    Committee of Trustees to receive money

      voted in, 1624,   III, 67a*

    patent for selling payments of, 1628(?),   III, 286b

Subsidy men, not to embark from Cinque

    Ports, 1634,   II, 92a (no. 4)*

Sugar; trade, 1612,   IV, 372b

    imports of, 1639,   Bath MSS., Vol. II, 75

Sundials,   VI, 461a

Surgeons; see: Physicians and surgeons.

Swain mote, proceedings in, at Waltham, co.

    Essex, 1604,   III, 211b

Tally Courts, records of,   VIII(3), 22a

Tapestries, bought of contractors for

    the late King's goods,   IX(2), 444b*

Taverns; see: Inns.

Taxation; levy of double tenth for Palatinate

    War, 1620,   II, 88a

    hidage, 1633,   II, 18b

    poll money; in co. Worcester, temp.

      Car. 1(?),   I, 55a

    —; in Bucks, 1640,   VII, 434b

Textile fabrics (cont.);

See also: Cloth trade; Silk; Wool.

Tiles, inventor's petition for patent for "pan"
    or Flanders tiles, 1636,   III, 191a
Tilting,   VII, 529a-b*

Tin, price of, 1643,   II, 99a
Tithes, farming of "small tithes"
    (calves, lambs, pigs), 1606,

                    Finch MSS., Vol. I, 38*
of Beechwood, 1632,   VII, 548b
compounding for, in King's forest of
    Exmoor, 1633,   VI, 472a
detained from R. Jones, 1645,   VIII(1), 7b
of Leighton, etc., 1646,   VIII(1), 11a*

Tobacco; 1603-1652,
           Rutland MSS., Vol. IV, 443-537, passim*
Northumberland's expenses for,
    1606-1616,   VI, 229-231, passim*
impositions on pipes and, imported into
    Ireland, 1631,   IV, 369b
opinions as to its being an "aliment,"
    1636,   V, 333b, 358b
annuity from, granted to Princess Elizabeth,
    1637,   I, 34b
manufacture and trade, 1616-1631, VIII(2), 31-49*
price of,   Egmont MSS., Vol. I, 388*
sale of; 1622,   VIII(2), 29b
—; licenses for, temp. Car. 1,   I, 34a

Tobacco (cont.);

from Association Island (Tortuga), 1634,

VII, 549a

See also: Colonies—Virginia.

Tobacco pipes, monopoly on, suppressed,

1621,   II, 59b (no. 369)

Tomb of Queen Elizabeth, payment for,

1607,   III, 264b

Tombs, upkeep of,   V, 410b

Tonnage and poundage, speech of Charles I

on, 1641,   III, 84a

Tower of London; stores supplied to,   III, 186a

offices and salaries, temp. Jac. 1,   VIII(3), 31a

expenses of Northumberland in, 1606-

1616,   VI, 229a-231a

accounts of, 1616, 1617,   VII, 671b, 672a, 673b

medicines to sick prisoners in,

1617,   VII, 673b

Lieutenant of; temp. Jac. 1,

VII, 671a-674b, passim;

VIII(1), 87a-89a, passim*

—; holding hostages, 1613,   VII, 670b*

—; Exchequer payment to, 1657(?),   VIII(1), 95a

Trade; letters and papers on,

Rutland MSS., Vol. IV, 447-541, passim*;

III, 213b, 253b; IV, 372b; VI, 351a

unlawful transportation of goods, 1620(?), III, 64b

letters by London merchants on, 1622,

1623, 1624,   III, 215b

Trade, foreign—With particular countries; Spain (cont.);

Trees; (cont.);

    1647,   Egmont MSS., Vol. I, 482*
   lime trees from Low Countries for
     Hyde Park, 1611-1612,   IX(2), 424b-425a*
   fruit trees brought from Chester,
    1653,   Egmont MSS., Vol. I, 531*
   "red wood tree" from (Old) Providence
    Island,   VII, 549a
   on Crown lands, in Forests, etc.; surveys
    and sales of woods,   IV, 334a; V, 407a, 416b
   —; felling of,   V, 403b

Trial by combat; Cheke-Dutton, 1609,   III, 295a
  See also: Duels.

Trials; 1603-1655,   III, 298a-b
  collection of State,   VIII(3), 22b
  of peers and peeresses for treason,
    conference as to,   I, 12b

Troops; see: Army and militia.
Tulip ("Tallopp" or "Tolepasse" root),   IX(2), 386a

Turkish pirates; see: Pirates.

Twelfth Night, cake for,   V, 390b

Universities—General; letters to J. Selden
  relating to,   V, 312a-b
  question of episcopal and archiepiscopal
   jurisdiction,   V, 313a, 407b
  petition to Vice Chancellor (of Oxford
   or Cambridge) about living of Kirkby

Universities—General (cont.);

Universities—Cambridge—General; Catalogue of

Universities—Cambridge—Colleges; Christ's

239

Universities—Oxford—Colleges (cont.);

Voyages and travel—Particular countries; Europe
(cont.);

—; Winchelsea, 1657-1658,

Finch MSS., Vol. I, 75-76*

France; G. Varney, 1609, IX(2), 386a

—; T. Wilbraham (?) with Sir T. Edmondes;
1614, III, 292b

—; —; 1625(?), III, 292b

—; Duke of Buckingham, 1617, I, 49a; VI, 326b

—; E. Filmer, 1640, III, 246a

—; T. White, 1652,

Egmont MSS., Vol. I, 508, 510-511*

—; Sir J. Cope, 1654, III, 244a

Germany; Earl of Shrewsbury's visit to
Bavaria, 1616-1618, Var. Coll. Vol. II, 312*

—; W. Gell in, 1638, IX(2), 390b

Guiana, Raleigh's expedition, 1617,
III, 185a, 204a, 214b, 215a, 353a; VI, 328b-329a, 362b;
VII, 592a; VIII(2), 32b*; IX(2), 386a

Hudson River, exploration of, 1623, VIII(2), 45b*

India, W. Smith (of Nibley) in, 1658-1660,
V, 360a-b

Indies; 1655, II, 83a

—; "passage toward" (letter of Raleigh),
21 Mar., 1617, V, 409b

Java, Sir Thomas Dale, 1618, VII, 673b

Narrow Seas, Sir R. Leveson and Sir W.
Monson, 1613(1603), VI, 301a, 305b

Netherlands, Sir T. Overbury's observations

Voyages and travel— Particular countries (cont.);

    on, 1619,   IX (2), 386a

    Northwest Passage; Spanish jealousy at

    English discovery of, 1612,   X (1), 576, 583*

    —; money from Prince for voyage to,

    1612,   VII, 670a-b

    Spain, visit of Sir R. Phelips (Spanish

    Match), (1615),   I, 59-60*

    Teneriffe, Mr. Clapham's voyage to, 1646,

                             VII, 515b

    Tetuan, J. Harrison's journey to, temp.

    Car. 1,   IV, 411a

    Virginia; 1619-1623,   V, 340b-341a

    —; agreement relating to voyage to,

    1605,   VIII (2), 31a*

    West Indies, Prince Rupert's expedition

    to, 1651-1653,   IX (2), 441b

Wages; assessed by justices of the peace, co.

    Lincoln; 1619,   XII (4), 455

    —; 1621,   XII (4), 460-462*

    of seamen, withheld by merchant

    captains,   VI, 285-286*

    to servants,   VI, 228-231, passim*;

               VI, 323b-324a*, 327b, 450a

    of "auncient bearer" (ensign bearer),

    1629,   V, 412b

    of Yeoman of the Robes to Charles I, 1649,

                          III, 265b

    See also: Fees; Household, Royal; Salaries.

Women (cont);

    riots by pro-Parliament, 1642,   VII, 439a*

Wood; bought and sold,

                V, 388a, 393b; VII, 669b; IX(2), 375b

    hedgerows to be cut, 1642,   V, 388a*

    repairing of rails in Henley

      Park, 1609,   VII, 669b

    taken by soldiers, to be restored, 1648,

                                V, 361a

    claimed as manorial right, 1656,   V, 304b

    See also: Trees.

Woods; see: Forests; Trees.

Wool; industry and trade; temp. Jac. 1,   III, 58b

    —; in Western counties, 1612(?)-1617(?),

                               III, 63b

    —; in Taunton, 1617(?),   III, 63b

    petition about seizure of cloths,

      1604(?),   III, 52b

    prices and payment for,   V, 387b, 391b, 395a;

                    Finch MSS., Vol. I, 42*

    baize, counterfeiting of seals for,

      1632,   III, 71a-b

    frieze, price of,   IV, 343a

Works, Office of, increase of prices of labor

    and material at, 1608,   VII, 669b

Writers, of the Court and Livery of the

    City of London, petition of, 1605(?),   VI, 223a

Writing; see: Penmanship; Scriveners.

APPENDIX A

Parliamentary Proceedings,
1621 to 10 January, 1642, in Print.

A Selective List
(exclusive of official journals)

1621

Notes of the debates in the House of Lords, officially
taken by Henry Elsing. . . A.D. 1621, edited. . .by
Samuel Rawson Gardiner, (Westminster), Camden Society,
1870. (Camden Society. Publications, no. 103)

Commons debates, 1621, (edited by) Wallace Notestein,
Frances Helen Relf (and) Hartley Simpson. New Haven,
Yale University Press; London, Oxford University
Press, 1935. (Yale historical publications. Manuscripts
and edited texts, XIV, i.e., XV, 7 vols.)

Proceedings and debates of the House of Commons,
in 1620 and 1621. Collected by a member of that
House (Sir Edward Nicholas). And now published
from his original manuscript, in the Library of
Queen's College, Oxford (by Thomas Tyrwhitt). With
an appendix: In which some passages are illustrated
from other manuscripts. . .Oxford, Clarendon Press,
1766. 2 vols.

The Hastings Journal of the Parliament of 1621 (House

of Lords), edited by Lady De Villiers. . .London,
Royal Historical Society, 1953. (Camden Miscellany,
vol. XX (no. 2))

Forms part of the Royal Historical Society's
Publications, Camden Third series, vol. LXXVIII.

By Henry Hastings, 5th Earl of Huntingdon.

1621, 1625, 1628

Notes of the debates in the House of Lords, officially
taken by Robert Bowyer and Henry Elsing. . .A.D.
1621, 1625, 1628, edited. . .by Frances Helen Relf.
London, Royal Historical Society, 1929. (Royal
Historical Society. Publications, Camden series. Third
series, vol. 42)

1624, 1626

Notes of the debates in the House of Lords, officially
taken by Henry Elsing. . .A.D. 1624 and 1626, edited
. . .by Samuel Rawson Gardiner. (Westminster),
Camden Society, 1879. (Camden Society. Publications,
new series, no. 24)

1625

Debates in the House of Commons in 1625, edited
from a MS. in the library of Sir Rainald Knightley,
Bart., by Samuel Rawson Gardiner. (Westminster,
Royal Historical Society), 1873. (Camden Society.
Publications, new series, no. 6)

Identified as by John Pym.

Draft journal and committee book of 1625 (In The
Manuscripts of the House of Lords, vol. XI (new

series) ... Addenda, 1514-1714, edited by Maurice
F. Bond ... London, H.M. Stationery Office, 1962,
p. 177-207)

1629

Commons debates for 1629, critically edited, and an
introduction dealing with parliamentary sources for the
early Stuarts, edited by Wallace Notestein and Frances
Helen Relf. Minneapolis, University of Minnesota,
1921. (University of Minnesota. Studies in the social
sciences, no. 10)

Corrections and additions to "A True Relation,"
p. 1-106 in this work, are listed in the following
article on Hunter MS. 52 in the Chapter Library at
Durham:

Hughes, Edward. A Durham manuscript of the
Commons debates of 1629. (In English Historical
Review, vol. LXXIV, 1959, p. 672-679)

1640-1642

D'Ewes, Sir Simonds, Bart. The journal of Sir
Simonds D'Ewes from the beginning of the Long
Parliament to the opening of the trial of the Earl of
Strafford, edited by Wallace Notestein. New Haven,
Yale University Press; London, Oxford University
Press, 1923. (Yale historical publications. Manu-
scripts and edited texts, VII)

D'Ewes, Sir Simonds, Bart. The journal of Sir
Simonds D'Ewes, from the first recess of the Long
Parliament to the withdrawal of King Charles from
London, edited by Willson Havelock Coates. New

Haven, Yale University Press; London, Oxford University Press, 1942. (Yale historical publications. Manuscripts and edited texts, XVIII)

The House of Lords Calendar of Manuscripts. List of volumes. (In The Manuscripts of the House of Lords vol. XI (new series) ... Addenda, 1514-1714 ... London, H. M. Stationery Office, 1962, p. 567-568)

Nos. 1-7, in Appendices to the First to Seventh Reports, cover the period to 1665. Under no. 4, 1625-1641, is noted "The Papers from now on practically follow the daily entries in the Lords' Journals."

The Commons Debates Project, which plans to publish eventually diaries for other Parliaments before 1640, is located at the University of California at Los Angeles.

APPENDIX B

List of Collections

Here are listed (a) the collections, and (b) the Inspectors' and the Commissioners' Reports that are within the scope of this Guide. If pages are noted it means that the items referred to in the Subject-Index are limited to single pages or a particular block of pages out of the total covered by the collection. Volumes not bearing numbers in the series of Reports are designated "Vol."

In many of the collections listed the items are few or widely scattered, and some collections may contain material additional to that represented in the Subject-Index.

A collection the name of which is in parentheses is one that has been destroyed.

Collection	Report
Almack	I
Arley Hall	III
Arundell, Lord, of Wardour	II, 34b
Ashburnham	VIII(3)
Baginton	II
Bagot (Blithfield MSS.)	IV
Bankes	VIII(1)